Padre Pio

Stories From Those Who Knew Him

Roberto Allegri

translated by Martina Adani

theWORD among us® *press*

© 2021 Ancora SRL
All rights reserved.

Published by The Word Among Us Press
7115 Guilford Drive, Suite 100
Frederick, Maryland 21704
wau.org

Originally published as *I miei diletti figliuoli* by Ancora Editrice in 2021.

27 26 25 24 23   1 2 3 4 5

ISBN: 978-1-59325-561-9
eISBN: 978-1-59325-563-3

Unless otherwise noted, Scripture texts in this work are taken from the *New American Bible, revised edition* © 2010, 1991, 1986, 1970 Confraternity of Christian Doctrine, Washington, D.C., and are used by permission of the copyright owner. All rights reserved. No part of the *New American Bible* may be reproduced in any form without permission in writing from the copyright owner.

Design by Suzanne Earl

No part of this publication may be reproduced, stored in a retrieval system, or transmitted in any form or by any means—electronic, mechanical, photocopy, recording, or any other—except for brief quotations in printed reviews, without the prior permission of the author and publisher.

Library of Congress Control Number: 2023906410

Contents

Introduction 7

1. "Time Had No Meaning." 12
2. "He Used to Call Me *Pitturì*." 18
3. Close to Mystery 23
4. An Oranges and Candies 28
5. A Body Made of Light 33
6. "Nobody Wants to Carry the Cross." 37
7. "Come on! What Have to Do Our Duty!" 43
8. His Eyes Pierced Your Soul 48
9. Butterflies and Little Birds 53
10. It Was Impossible Not to
    Fall in Love with Him 57
11. Little Presents in the Pockets 61
12. Violets and Incense Scent 65
13. "God Give You Back a Hundred;
    a Thousand Doubles for One." 69
14. Kisses on the Cheeks 73
15. Goat Milk 78

16. Always in Dialect 83

17. "I Used to Pull His Beard." 87

18. Friendly Jokes 91

19. Artichokes of Pietrelcina 96

20. A Holy Cousin 99

21. Touching Tenderness 104

22. "Go in Peace! I Already Know Everything!" 107

23. Head Bowed, Rosary in Hand 110

24. "Our Lady Knows What to Do." 115

25. "I Think of Him When I Celebrate Mass." 119

26. "Did You Dare to Doubt?" 123

27. "Be Quiet, Agostì! Do Not Worry!" 127

28. Never Far from Him 131

29. A Seal on the Soul 135

30. The Spiritual Children's Needs 139

31. "This Is the Friar I See!" 143

32. Padre Pio's Sugared Almonds 147

33. "You Made Me Look Ugly!" 151

34. The Last Goodbye 156
35. "Jesus Wants You to Be a Priest." 160
36. "Everything Will Be Alright." 164
37. He Was Different from the Others 169
38. The Work of the Soul 173
39. Letters from All Over the World 177
40. Eel and Turnip Greens 181
41. Wedding with a Miracle 186
42. A Foretaste of Heaven 190
43. "If You Do Not Want Me Here,
    I Will Leave." 194
44. Jesus' Photocopy 198
45. The Politician's Funeral 202
46. "When Are You Going to
    Bring Me Your Boy?" 206
47. The Child and the Saint 209

Introduction

I have heard about Padre Pio ever since I was a child. My father, Renzo Allegri, who worked as a journalist, met him in 1967 on assignment as a special reporter for the Italian magazine *Gente*. It turned out to be a special encounter since, following that assignment, most of my father's works have focused on that mysterious friar who lived in the Gargano area. I grew up listening to the stories my father told me about him. I remember that my father would always get emotional. Even today, when my father talks about Padre Pio, he has a special light on his face, like the light at dawn, full of promises and sweetness.

"I met Padre Pio in April 1967," my father told me. "He was old and very sick. He died the following year. What impressed me the most were not the wonders he worked that people would talk. It was rather the strength released by his personality, a moral strength that was visible. I saw him walking towards me, bent in the hallway of the monastery. His feet must have felt like lead; he was limping and leaning on the walls so that he would not fall. It was sad to see him walking in those conditions. I could feel his sufferings; I could understand how deep his pain was. However, he did not complain. He was indeed willing to help those who needed it most. And then there was his gaze. When he raised his head and looked at you, his eyes were on fire. But at the same time, they were so full of kindness that they made you speechless.

I was in San Giovanni Rotondo for work, and I had my camera with me. When I was close enough to him, I took some pictures, but the flash blinded him. He shouted, 'Stop it!' The look on his face was scary. All he wanted was to pray and have a quiet existence. I had no idea that there were other people, such as interfering photographers, who were trying to find out rumors about his life. I said to him, 'Father, I am just doing my job.' All of a sudden, he was appeased, as if the wind had blown on his face, calming him down. He came close to me, leaned on me, and asked me to go with him. I was holding him up; I was carrying him. I realized how painful his feet must have felt. Some people said that he had developed stigmata on his feet, even though not many people knew about it. He was undoubtedly suffering. Padre Pio was a man who suffered tremendously, enduring his pain like a hero.

"A short time before meeting Padre Pio, I had met Fr. Mario Mason, a Jesuit who told me how, in 1959, Our Lady of Fatima had miraculously healed Padre Pio. Nowadays the episode is well-known, but back then no one knew about it. That year, Padre Pio was ill, and he had not left his cell for several months. At that time, the statue of Our Lady of Fatima was being carried on a pilgrimage, and it was taken to the most important Italian dioceses. The statue was carried to the monastery of San Giovanni Rotondo, where it was kept for two days thanks to some of Padre Pio's friends. Despite his health issues, Padre Pio managed to pray in front of the statue, which was later helicoptered to its next destination. Padre Pio saw it through a window and said, '*Madonnina*, when you got here, I was sick. Now you are about to leave, and I am still sick . . . ' Suddenly he started shaking. It looked like a current went straight through his body, and he was instantly healed. Fr. Mason had told me about that episode, and on that day in April, when I met Padre Pio, I wanted to ask him about it. As soon as I mentioned the episode, he burst into tears. He was sobbing like a child, and he mumbled 'Yes, yes, I recovered thanks to Our Lady . . . !' Later, the father superior of the monastery explained to me that each time Padre Pio tried to talk about his recovery, he would get emotional and cry, and be unable to finish his story."

I guess Padre Pio and my father discussed other topics, but I never found out about them. It belongs to my father's personal life, and I do not wish to cross the line. My father's career focused on writings about Padre Pio. He published hundreds of articles and dozens of books. This shows that something must have happened during their meeting. As the next pages will demonstrate, all those who met Padre Pio were positively affected by him. My father kept saying that, despite his sufferings, Padre Pio was a role model when it came to optimism: he believed in the future. According to my father, "He was and keeps being a hopeful man. In spite of severe difficulties throughout his life, Padre Pio always infused people with love and trust. He never stopped; his faith was so solid. . . . He believed in progress, and the hospital conceived by him was, since its opening, ahead of its time. Above all, Padre Pio was the embodiment of God's mercy. He was really affectionate, and he loved people. He used to cry with the desperate ones and laugh with those that were happy. Some people claim that his manners were abrupt. One day, one of his brothers, Fr. Pellegrino, complained about it. Padre Pio told him, 'I act this way because I do not want emotions to overpower me. I am about to cry when I meet people who are suffering, and I would not be able to keep doing my job.'"

But what was it like to talk to Padre Pio? How did it feel when you looked in his eyes and when he looked back at you? How was his voice? And how did he use to pray? What was it like to watch him celebrating Mass while he was limping? What did his stigmata look like? And then, how was Padre Pio's daily life in the monastery? What was his schedule? What did he like to eat and drink? Is it true that he liked tobacco?

These are some of the questions about Padre Pio that I have always asked myself. These questions are not related to my job as a journalist. Nor do I wish to explain his personality to readers because I believe it would be impossible to illustrate a saint. The reason behind these questions is that I feel envious of the people who had the privilege of meeting him and being close to him. This makes me ask these people: please, tell me all the details! The more details I have, the easier it is to envision Padre Pio next to me, here and now.

I have read many books about Padre Pio to find the answers to these questions. I especially enjoy reading the books that were published while he was still alive by people who were close to him and whose feelings were sincere. They are important books that convey the beauty of being in contact with a saint. They are brave books as well because back then, part of the Church opposed Padre Pio, and it was therefore risky to share certain opinions, especially if you were a religious person. However, his personality was too intense, and people could not be silenced. Many of them felt the urgency to share with the world the wonders they had witnessed and that were occurring thanks to that bearded friar who lived in the Gargano area.

Nevertheless, these books were not enough for me. Something was missing: it was the gaze and the voice of those who had met Padre Pio in person. It is different to perceive the excitement in the people's voices, to listen to their memories, to see the trembling light in their eyes full of tears. It is different to feel the hands of the witnesses, clasping your arm while they tell you their stories because they want to assure you they are telling the truth, and they wish to instill their emotions in you. I was looking for these people: Padre Pio's friends, the ones he talked with, those who held him up while he was walking. I was also looking for those individuals who had only met him once, but that meeting was enough to change them, to receive a gift, to be shaken.

Padre Pio died more than fifty years ago. Most of his friends are no longer with us. The people who met him or that simply attended his Mass are now old. We risk losing these precious experiences. We also risk losing that light in the gaze of these people, which shows the sweetness of the truth. These stories need to be kept and saved. I have been writing about Padre Pio for twenty years. I had the chance to talk to many people, and I have gathered together several stories. Most of these people have died, but I managed to listen to them in time. When it was not possible to talk with the witnesses, I spoke with their children or grandchildren, and I found out that their memories about Padre Pio were passed on within the family.

In the next pages, you will find what I was told by friends and brothers, relatives, men and women who had met Padre Pio when they were children growing up near the monastery, and also by doctors, artists, journalists, and pilgrims who came to San Giovanni Rotondo looking for consolation. Each one of them, as with an imaginary paintbrush, added a personal touch to the painting that portrays a great saint. They say, with their moved voices, "I met him."

1

"Time Had No Meaning."

"Padre Pio was the one looking for me, like a father who looks for his child. It was July 1947, and I was seventeen years old. I went to San Giovanni Rotondo for the first time, and it turned out to be an overwhelming experience, the most all-encompassing experience of my life. From that moment, Padre Pio has never left me alone. He is always close to me. He never abandons me."

Mrs. Ida Bartolucci radiates such an explosive peace of mind; it hits you like a gust of wind. She is ninety years old, but she doesn't look it. Her manners and the way she speaks are elegant, and her gaze is very sweet. She has always been a housewife. She raised four children, and for thirty years, she has been taking people to Padre Pio's grave on pilgrimages. She lives in a beautiful place. Belvedere Fogliense is a little village in the hills surrounding Urbino. The silence here is almost absolute, and the landscape makes your heart sing. Mrs. Ida immediately agrees to tell me about her meeting with Padre Pio, with a tissue in her hands, because she can't talk about him without getting emotional.

"In 1947, the war had been over for two years, and people wanted to find a job and move on with their lives. Nobody talked about Padre Pio. Only a few people knew him, and even fewer had met him. At that time, I lived in Rome with my parents, and I worked in a wool factory. One of my friends went to Apulia on her honeymoon. Somebody told her about a friar who lived in the Gargano area, so she went to San Giovanni Rotondo. She was impressed. She brought me a gift: it was a little book, very small, with Padre Pio's picture on the cover. The size was that of a passport photo. However, there was a whole mountain within that square inch: it magnetized me. I looked at it, at Padre Pio's picture, and I felt the need to go there. To him. I tried to deny it. I told myself it was a long trip, that I was too young, and it could be dangerous. But it was useless. It looked like Padre Pio was calling me, and his call was too intense. I decided to travel with a friend of mine so that I would not be alone. We waited for the factory to give us a three days' leave, and we left for Apulia. When I saw Padre Pio, right there in front of me, I was overwhelmed by an unbelievable power.

"Padre Pio celebrated Mass at five in the morning, but you had to wait in line at four o'clock. We were all standing in line, in the darkness, in front of the closed door of the monastery. Then, at the time of the celebration, the doors were opened, and the pilgrims filled the little church, trying to get as close as possible to Padre Pio. On that day, I saw him celebrating Mass, and I actually understood its meaning. I have never forgotten it. His Mass was a mystery, so deep and mystical. It has been stated on different occasions, and it has been written about in many books, that during Mass, Padre Pio's body lived through Christ's Passion again. And it was true; I witnessed it. Padre Pio suffered physically, and everyone could see it. I saw his face crumpling, with his staring eyes, and his mouth seemed to be about to scream. It was hard for him to breathe, he attempted to stand, and he leaned on the altar. His face was covered with sweat and tears. It was heart-wrenching; we were all witnesses of a torture. The people were on their knees, crying. Everybody was suffering together with him. It felt like the sufferings were never going to end, but then it was time for the Consecration. Padre Pio raised the host, and he held it with his outstretched arms. Some people say he could hold it up for half an hour. He did the same with the goblet. He was ecstatic again and again during Mass. He used to suddenly look up and start talking to someone only he could see. Watching a man going into ecstasies is overwhelming: he is made of light, and you are aware of his soul leaving his body. Mass lasted more than two hours, but none of the people felt the exhaustion or the pain in their legs after all that time kneeling. Everybody was focusing on Padre Pio, on the sacrifice he was experiencing. Time no longer had a meaning. Later, following Holy Communion, Padre Pio was different; he became bright and peaceful. We could all notice his spiritual joy. I have no doubts: watching him was like watching Jesus.

"I did not manage to talk to him on that occasion, in 1947. There was no time; I had to go back to work. If you wished to confess to Padre Pio, you had to book him in advance, and the wait could last days. Even though I did not have the opportunity to talk to him, when I was back home, I felt different. I had lived a one-of-a-kind experience. I really thought that the monastery was my future and that I was going to become a nun. But God had different plans for me. I went to Pesaro on vacation, and I met Matteo, who later became my husband. I was in love, but I was hesitating. I did not know if the right choice was to accept his courting or to devote myself to God. One night I had a dream: I was in a room with two of my previous suitors that I had rejected. Suddenly, Matteo was also there, and I heard a very sweet voice that said, 'This one is for you.'

"I woke up, and I had no doubts. Matteo and I were married in 1952, and we immediately visited Padre Pio to be blessed.

"I remember it as if it happened yesterday. He was in the confessional, which was open because he could not breathe normally, and he needed fresh air. Matteo and I were newlyweds. We bent on our knees, in front of him. My joined hands were on Padre Pio's legs, and he kindly looked at us, smiling. I was surrounded by a beautiful floral scent, similar to a dense scented fog. It was an indescribable moment. I told him, 'Father, we are on our honeymoon. We ask you for your blessing, both for us and for our families at home.' He opened his arms and looked up to the sky. 'Congratulations! May God help you with your new family. May he grant you several children.' His words, his deep voice, the sweetness of his tone: I can still feel all of it if I think about it, even now.

"Then, Padre Pio put his hands on our heads, and that was the most significant moment. I can't tell you the happiness I felt at that time; it is impossible to describe it. It was not an earthly happiness, but it was rather coming from heaven, I am sure. It was too uplifting. He gave us his hand so that we could kiss it. I gently took it between my hands, and I noticed that there was a hole on its back, where the bones were supposed to be. The glove that covered his hand was so thin that I could easily see the wound beneath it. I kissed his hand twice. I was holding it, and it took me a while before sharing it with my husband. As I said, it was an amazing experience. Unforgettable.

"Our life together began, and it was not easy. My husband was not doing well. During the Second World War, he had been a prisoner of war in Germany, an experience that had deeply affected him. Matteo was suffering from a severe depression, but it was not considered an illness back then. Doctors did not know how to handle it. He was depressed, and I was pregnant with our fourth child. We were poor, but I still trusted God. That is why I often used to sing: to distract Matteo from his gloomy thoughts and to share my good mood with the children. However, we are weak creatures, and we easily fall apart. One night indeed, I was too discouraged, and I burst into tears. But suddenly, something occurred to me. I remembered that Padre Pio had told his spiritual children to send their guardian angel to him when they were scared. I decided to do it. I went to my bedroom, and I started praying, 'My Guardian Angel, go visit Padre Pio. Ask him if he can heal my husband and if he can find us a job. Please, ask him also to help me with my pregnancy.'

"Three days later the postman came by with a letter for me from San Giovanni Rotondo. It was strange because I did not know anyone from there, so nobody could have my address. I opened it. It was handwritten by Angelo Battisti, the administrator of the hospital *Casa Sollievo della Sofferenza*. It was the answer to my prayers. He wrote, 'Dear Mrs., Padre Pio asked me to inform you that he will pray for you, for your husband's health, and for the finances of your family. He sends you his blessings.' In a short time, our lives changed. My husband got better, and soon after that, an unexpected job improved our family's situation. However, I still had to deal with my difficult pregnancy. The doctors thought I would not be able to give birth. But one night I had a dream. There was a friar with his brown tunic, and a voice told me, 'You are suffering, but do not worry. You will have a good son, who will travel around the world.' A few days later, Stefano was born. He is a famous musician now, he constantly travels around the world, as I was told in my dream. Every day he brings the beauty of music somewhere.

"This is my story. The least I could do to reciprocate Padre Pio's loving presence was to take the pilgrims to him. I keep doing it. It is tiring but I am happy. I know he is happy, too. Five years ago, I led a group of pilgrims with more than a hundred people. When we left the cathedral in San Giovanni Rotondo, I saw a friar among the crowd. It was Padre Pio! I immediately recognized him because of his beard, his cowl, and his slow pace. I followed him and stopped in front of him. I cried out, 'You are Padre Pio!' He did not deny it. With his hand, he made the sign of the cross and answered, 'God bless you!'"

2

"He Used to Call Me *Pitturì*."

On a beautiful autumn day, I went to Florence to meet Antonio Ciccone. The sky was so clear; it felt like being in a painting. We decided to meet in his workshop in the center of Florence. It is a sunny attic full of paintings. Antonio is usually reluctant to talk about himself, but when I explained to him on the phone that I wanted to talk about Padre Pio, he did not hesitate.

Antonio was born in San Giovanni Rotondo in 1939, and he is now a famous international artist. He was one of Pietro Annigoni's students, and he put on more than two hundred personal exhibitions in Europe and in the United States, where he lived for almost fifteen years. Most of his works focus on Padre Pio. Many of them can be found at *Casa Sollievo della Sofferenza*, in the monastery, and in different locations in San Giovanni Rotondo. Some of them belong to important collections in Great Britain and in the United States. Between 1986 and 1987, Antonio displayed his works on Padre Pio and on the nature of Gargano in the UK and Ireland. I was told that he had known Padre Pio very well when he was a child and that the friar was precisely the one who encouraged him to study art.

Once I got comfortable in a room with a big painting of Padre Pio holding the rosary, Antonio told me, "I owe him everything. Thanks to him I had the chance to study. When I was a child, I was a shepherd in San Giovanni Rotondo, but when I was seven years old, I discovered the joy of drawing. From that moment, all I wanted to do was to become an artist. However, my family did not have the means to support me, so I asked Padre Pio for advice. He smiled at me and said, 'God's Providence will help you soon.' And it was true."

Antonio wore a beret on his head, round glasses, and a green scarf around his neck. He had long hair. He watched me closely before sharing his story with me. I could not tell if he was interested in my face from an artistic point of view or if he was trying to understand something, such as if he could tell me about his childhood. His smile revealed his decision.

"Elvira Serritelli was my first and second grade teacher in elementary school. She was one of Padre Pio's spiritual children. She took me to church early in the morning so that I could see the friar everybody was talking about. I began to confess to him. I remember that sometimes he was very sweet, while on other occasions, he was harsh and almost scary. One day, in the confessional, he frightened me by asking, 'Were the cherries tasty?' I felt so embarrassed. While I had been grazing the cows in the countryside, I had stolen several cherries, and I had eaten them. No one had noticed me, but Padre Pio knew everything.

"Then, drawing began to fascinate me. I was drawing all the time, everywhere, using different tools, such as pieces of charcoal or brick fragments. In the early 1950s, I started drawing portraits of Padre Pio. I used to spy on him during Mass. I observed his face when I confessed to him, and I would later depict him at home or in the stable, when I was with my donkey. I remember that once, I had not even knelt down yet when he sent me away.

He knew I was there merely to observe his face so that I could later draw it. I was fascinated by his face, his gaze, his bushy eyebrows, his beard. His face showed a strong personality. Even though I was just a child, I really wanted to portray his facial features. However, Padre Pio never posed. Therefore, I had to observe him closely, and I had to memorize all the details so that I could remember them later. Once I was so insistent that Padre Pio eventually decided to pose. He simply did me a favor, and he could not wait until I finished. One day, I gathered some of my drawings and sketches, as well as a few watercolors, and I brought them to him. I wanted to ask him for advice. I wished to study art, but my family could not afford it, and I wanted to find out Padre Pio's opinion.

"One of my works that I was showing him was a copy of the crucifixion painting by Guercino. He looked at it intensely. Then, he put his hand on my hand and said, 'Be patient; God's Providence will help you soon. In the meantime, keep praying.' A year went by. There was a parish priest in Florence, don Benedetto Ricci, who was from San Giovanni Rotondo. When he came back to his village, Padre Pio appointed him to take some of my drawings to Florence, in order to show them to a few experts. One of these works was a colorful portrayal of Padre Pio. Once in Florence, don Ricci kept my drawings on a table in his house. One day, the Fancelli couple, who were both Padre Pio's spiritual children, stopped by don Ricci's house. They noticed Padre Pio's portrait on the table, and they were impressed. They asked don Ricci who the artist was, and he explained to them that it was a young man from San Giovanni Rotondo who really hoped to study art. The Fancelli couple suggested then to take my works to Pietro Annigoni, a great artist from Milan, who was already famous at that time, an actual *mostro sacro*. When Annigoni gave a look at my drawings, he said, 'This young man has some potential, but he needs to forget everything and start all over again.' The Fancelli couple were happy to hear his opinion, and somehow they also felt responsible for sponsoring me. For this reason, they decided to let me live with them in Florence so that I could study. However, they first talked with Padre Pio about it. He smiled and told them, 'Of course! God bless you!'

"It was a dream come true. Florence was an artistic center; it was all I had wished for. Before leaving, I said goodbye to Padre Pio. I wanted to thank him because I knew he had prayed for me. He said 'See? God's Providence helped you. Go, and God bless you. Behave!' It was 1954. I was about to start a new life. In Florence I even studied with Professor Nerina Simi, the daughter of the great painter Filadelfo Simi. She was also a superb artist. At the same time, I was welcomed to Annigoni's workshop. It was a difficult but amazing school. In the 1960s, an art dealer from Palm Beach, Florida, got in touch with me. He took some of my works with him, and he noticed that the American audience appreciated them. He invited me to put on an exhibition in the United States, after which I became popular. When I told Padre Pio I was leaving for the United States, he blessed me and fatherly warned me: 'Be careful! Do not make a bad impression!'

"I was always in touch with him. I visited him every year. He used to ask me, 'How are you doing, *pitturì* (little painter)?' Once, the friars of San Giovanni asked me to take care of some frescoes in the monastery. I remember a strange episode. I was working on the highest wall of a huge hall, on top of a scaffolding. All of a sudden, my foot was in the wrong position, and I lost my balance. I should have crashed into the ground, but something extraordinary took place. I felt confident, and I was not afraid. Like an acrobat, I nimbly stretched my arm, and I firmly grabbed the scaffolding. I did not understand how I had been able to do that. I looked below, and Padre Pio was there, staring at me. It all made sense then. I am sure he protected me. I have to admit that I always perceived his presence next to me. I could even smell his scent, even when I was far away in Florence or in the United States. When I felt discouraged or when I was going through a hard time, I immediately perceived his typical sweet scent, which made me believe in myself.

"When Padre Pio died, I was in Southampton, New York. I learned the news from the newspapers. It is still difficult to describe my feelings. I was clearly sad, but I truly believed that Padre Pio was there, next to me. I got goose bumps. Since his death, the way I paint and portray him has changed. My works are now more mature, more spiritual. Padre Pio is always next to me, and he guides me and encourages me with his Christian strength."

3

Close to Mystery

"I was lucky enough to meet Padre Pio. I did not forget his gaze because it was so powerful. There was pain in his eyes. His pain was a light that lit up the soul."

This is what Ottaviano Ottaviani told me. He lives in Fossombrone, in the province of Pesaro and Urbino. He is seventy-eight years old, and he is now retired, but he used to be an insurance agent. He has been married to his wife, Marta, for fifty-six years, and they have five daughters and seven grandchildren. He attended the monastery of San Giovanni Rotondo from 1963 until 1968. "Being around Padre Pio was overwhelming. I can't think of other words to better describe how I felt inside in those moments. Being around him meant moving closer to a great mystery. But at the same time, every kind of doubt or fear would disappear when I was next to him because he was extremely peaceful."

Ottaviano's smile is priceless. When you see it, you are sure it comes straight from his heart. The way he talks about Padre Pio, his enthusiasm, and the sweetness when he describes him are so engaging that while I listen to him, I feel like I am being cradled. It is like being under covers, under a blanket, while it is snowing outside.

"My first memory of Padre Pio dates back to when I was thirteen years old. I remember my mother at home, going up the stairs. She opened her right hand, where there was a small crucifix. One of Padre Pio's spiritual children had given it to her. She looked radiant and said, 'I smell a violet's scent. . . . It is everywhere in the house. . . . It is Padre Pio's scent!'

"Padre Pio became part of my family in 1957, when my aunt Iole got sick. She had pneumonia and typhus fever. She was feeling very bad, her temperature was high, around 40 degrees Celsius (104 degrees Fahrenheit), and it did not seem to go down. The doctors did not believe she would make it. Her mother, my grandmother Maria, was very devout. She repeatedly prayed to Padre Pio. As he suggested, she used to send her guardian angel to him. One night, something inexplicable happened. My aunt Iole saw Padre Pio sitting on the left side of her bed. He was calm and smiling. But her vision was more complex.

"My aunt told us that she had seen some flames on the wall next to her bed, like a sudden fire in her bedroom, while Padre Pio was on the opposite side. However, she was fascinated by the flames, rather than by Padre Pio. She stretched her hand in their direction. She was surprised to find that they did not emanate heat, but they were rather cool. They made her burned skin feel better. Then she heard Padre Pio's voice that said, 'These are the souls of Purgatory.' At the same time, another voice coming from the flames said, 'We are the holy souls of Purgatory.' My aunt felt serene and in good health, and she fell asleep. When she woke up, she had recovered. The fever had disappeared, and her temperature was around 36.5 degrees Celsius (97.7 Fahrenheit). The scent of jasmine filled the air in the room. When the nurse who was taking care of my aunt walked into the room, she was surprised. She exclaimed, 'Iole, you put on some perfume!' My aunt thought she was joking. The scent was really intense, but she probably could not smell it because she was surrounded by it. The doctor came and acknowledged her recovery. No following complications occurred.

"In 1963, my father moved from Ferrara to the Montedison in Brindisi, where he was in charge of the factory outlet. So we all moved to Apulia. We were no longer far from San Giovanni Rotondo. One day, my father took us to Padre Pio's Mass. I remember the previous sleepless night because we had to leave very early, before sunrise. The closer we got to Gargano, the more excited we were. The church was crowded, and everyone was there for his Mass. On that day I realized what mystery is, and since then, Padre Pio has never left my heart. I visited him often. Once I even stayed there for eight days. Something amazing happened that week.

"I read a book that mentioned an event that impressed me. A group of pilgrims were on their way to San Giovanni Rotondo. They all asked their guardian angels to deliver their requests to Padre Pio. When he saw them the following day, he told them, 'You are finally here! Your guardian angels did not let me sleep all night!' Padre Pio really insisted on the existence and help of guardian angels. In the letters he wrote to his devotees, he often encouraged them to turn to their guardian angels. He used to write, 'Send your guardian angel to me because it does not need a train ticket, and it won't wear out its shoes.'

"In a letter he wrote to his spiritual director, Fr. Agostino da San Marco, he explains to him that his own guardian angel woke him up early every morning in order to pray with him. 'When I close my eyes at night, I see heaven ahead of me,' he wrote. 'This vision delights me. I feel calm, and I fall asleep with a sweet smile on my face, waiting for my little childhood friend to wake me up so that we can say the morning prayers together.' Padre Pio would always say to his devotees, 'When you need me but you can't visit me, send your guardian angel to me with your message.' One day, one of these devotees asked him. 'Can you really hear what my guardian angel has to say to you?' Padre Pio answered, 'Well, do you think I am deaf?'

"After reading about these episodes, I decided to try something. While I was in San Giovanni Rotondo every day for a week, I hid myself behind a column of the church. I prayed to my guardian angel, and I sent it to Padre Pio. I said to it, 'Go … now!' In that exact moment, Padre Pio looked at me. I did it several times, and he always turned around, looking in my direction. On Sunday, after the Angelus and after blessing the faithful, I sent my guardian angel to him for the umpteenth time. Padre Pio burst out loudly, 'What do you want? What do you want from me?' He looked at me even though the church was overcrowded. I explained to him everything when I confessed to him, and he smiled.

"I remember another episode that took place during those days. While I was having dinner at my hotel, I saw a man sitting at a table near mine. He was emaciated, pale, and he had bags under his eyes. There was a big plate of pasta on the table in front of him, and I thought he was never going to eat it all. The owner of the hotel told me that the man had arrived in the morning, close to death. He had terminal stomach cancer. He was lying still on a stretcher, but then Padre Pio told him to get up. He immediately recovered, and now he was very hungry.

"What impressed me the most about Padre Pio was his modesty. He believed he was a sinner like all of us. I remember that when he said, '*Mea culpa, mea maxima culpa*' during Mass, he hit his chest so vigorously that you could hear it resounding everywhere in the church. He did not like to be the center of attention. Once I even heard him threatening to call the police if people did not stop calling him a saint.

"There was another occurrence. It was 1966, and my eldest daughter, Maria Raffaella, was one year old. The right side of her face suddenly began to swell. We took her to the Sant'Orsola hospital in Bologna because we were so worried. The medical examinations lasted two months. The doctors eventually diagnosed her with parotid gland cancer. She needed surgery, but it would be complicated. It was the first surgery of that kind in Italy and the second one in all of Europe. Surgeons came from abroad. There were many risks, and the doctors told me that even if my daughter survived, she would be scarred forever.

"My wife took our daughter to Mass every day, and she implored the Virgin Mary's pity. I prayed to Padre Pio, who was still alive. I sent my guardian angel to him, like I had done in the past. And on the day of the surgery, something unbelievable happened. The best cancer hospital in Italy had diagnosed my daughter with a tumor, and there were no doubts about it. During the surgery, however, the surgeons found a lipoma instead of a tumor, and they removed it. The surgery should have lasted twelve hours, but after only one hour, the doctors came out with tears in their eyes. They could not understand how a tumor could turn into a lipoma, but it happened. My daughter has always been in good health since then. Now she is married and has three children."

4

An Orange and Candies

"I was one of Padre Pio's altar boys," engineer Michele Grifa says. "He is part of all my childhood memories. I was born in San Giovanni Rotondo. I lived 200 meters (650 feet) away from the monastery, and I went there every day. Together with other children, I helped him in the afternoon with the Rosary and Vespers, as well as on Sunday during Mass. If I close my eyes, I can still see him: he moved slowly, limping. When we were too agitated, he kindly clipped us round the ear. He smiled at us like a father and looked at us with his sweet eyes. His gaze embraced us. For the children of San Giovanni Rotondo, Padre Pio represented the everyday life, and he was a pillar during our growth."

Engineer Grifa is sixty-six years old and lives in Viterbo, where he started his own business. I wanted to talk to him because of his experience as one of Padre Pio's altar boys. I wanted to understand what it was like to be so close to him during Mass, which was the most important part of the day for the friar.

"I felt strong emotions serving as an altar boy, and this affected me. When I was a young man, I chose to attend the seminary because I wanted to become a friar. But Padre Pio already knew that it was not my destiny. He always knew everything.

"As I said, we lived near the monastery. Therefore, we often turned to Padre Pio for every kind of issue: if we needed his advice, his encouragement, or his blessing. My father, Giovanni, for example, came back home once the war was over. He had also been a prisoner of war. He immediately confessed to Padre Pio. 'You are finally back!' Padre Pio said. And he added, 'So tell me, have you killed anyone?' My father answered that he was a soldier, and he had to use a weapon sometimes. 'Well, luckily you are not very good at shooting,' Padre Pio said. This comment was very important to my father because it assured him he had not killed anyone. That is what Padre Pio's comment meant.

"Those were difficult times, and poverty was common. There were no jobs, and working in the countryside was not profitable. My father decided to leave for Germany, like many others were doing. My mother was worried about being alone. She talked to Padre Pio about it, and he reassured her. 'There are so many things to do here in San Giovanni ... Do not worry; your husband will come back home!' The following month, my father found a job at the local hospital, *Casa Sollievo della Sofferenza*, where he worked until he retired. So he was always close to his family.

"One of my first memories of Padre Pio dates back to 1959, when I was five years old. It was July 1, and Padre Pio inaugurated the new church, Santa Maria delle Grazie. It was the new church he had wished for. He was involved in the construction, and he had chosen the architect. The original church of the monastery that was there in 1916 when he arrived in San Giovanni Rotondo was too small. It could no longer welcome all the people that attended Mass, and on several occasions, Padre Pio had had to celebrate Mass outside. The new church was big and spacious, and it was the place where he spent most of his time until he died. When it was inaugurated, there were so many people, including important ones, and they all paid homage to him. I remember I was holding my father's hand, and my new shoes were squeaking as I walked.

"I have another memory from those days. My father used to go out at night. Together with other men, he patrolled the streets to avoid Padre Pio being carried off. I did not understand it at that time, but later I found out that the Vatican often gave orders to take Padre Pio away from San Giovanni Rotondo. They never managed to do it because the people were strongly opposed.

"In the evening, with many other people from our village, we used to go outside of Padre Pio's cell, waiting for him to look out of the window and to greet the faithful, shaking his handkerchief. Other times, with my friends, we ran in the hallways of the monastery or in the basement of the church, where the crypt was being dug. The friars scolded us and told us that one day Padre Pio's grave would be there. But I did not believe them: I thought that Padre Pio would never die.

"When I was six years old, I became one of his altar boys. I usually went to the monastery to play around four in the afternoon, together with my classmates, and in the evening, for the Rosary and the Vespers. On those occasions and also on Sunday, during Mass, we helped Padre Pio. When I was next to him, I could often notice his stigmata because when it was time for the Consecration, he took off the gloves that were hiding his wounds. I saw the blood, the dark palms. Sometimes a few ruby red drops dripped. We were not particularly surprised because we were used to it. We had no idea of the meaning of those sores. We can assert that we were used to the supernatural. If I think about it now, I have the shivers.

"Sometimes, the other altar boys and I were distracted. In those cases, Padre Pio's face became surly, and he scolded us. He occasionally clipped us round the ear, but he did not really mean to be bad. He did not even have much strength because of the sores on his hands. When we saw his serious gaze, we immediately toed the line. Above all, we were sorry to upset him. His gaze was always friendly and affectionate, even when he frowned at us. One day, Padre Pio gave me an orange and some candies, and I took them home. I felt like I had found a treasure, and I happily showed them to my mother. I ate the orange, and it was very tasty. I have never eaten such a tasty orange after that one. I shared the candies with my sisters.

"Padre Pio was there when I received my First Communion. And he was there for my sisters. At that time, it was common to receive First Communion at seven years old. My youngest sister, who was named Pia in honor of Padre Pio, was too young for her First Communion because she was only six years old. But Padre Pio insisted. He asked my parents, 'What are you waiting for? It is the right time!' He was aware of my sister's spirituality more than anybody else. He thought she was mature enough to receive Holy Communion, and my parents trusted him and agreed. Pia got ready in one month, and she received her First Communion in July of 1968. Padre Pio died two months later. It seems like he wanted my sister to receive her First Communion before his death.

"After all those years spent in the monastery close to Padre Pio, I thought that maybe I could become a monk, too. My vocation was not very strong, and I later changed my mind. But when I was ten years old, I actually believed that was my destiny. I talked to Padre Pio about it, and I told him I wanted to go to Pietrelcina for the seminary. He smiled at me: 'Go! But you will be back!' Apparently, he already knew that I would change my mind. After my last year of high school, I realized indeed that I was not meant for that kind of life. I had finished a year of novitiate in Morcone, where Padre Pio had also been a novice in 1903. But I understood

I had to do something different, so I enrolled in college and became an engineer.

"When Padre Pio died on September 23, 1968, I was still attending the seminary. I remember I was woken up at sunrise, and I heard those terrible words: 'Michele, hurry up; Padre Pio has died!' We all went to San Giovanni Rotondo to go to the funeral. At that time, I could feel the painful but not permanent loss. Even though I could not see him, I knew Padre Pio was next to me. I could always feel his presence next to me. I often smelled his flower scent. I smelled it suddenly, not under specific circumstances. It still happens nowadays, and it gives me incredible courage and serenity."

5

A Body Made of Light

Professor Mario Spallone was a famous surgeon who died in 2013 at the age of ninety-six. He was the doctor for Palmiro Togliatti, Pietro Nenni, Giorgio Amendola, Nilde Jotti, Luigi Longo and other well-known members of the Italian left-wing political parties. Given his education and his mindset, he was not really into religion. Nevertheless, when I met him in his studio in Rome, one of the first things he told me was, "Padre Pio has always been a constant figure throughout my life. I am one of his devotees."

These words are impressive. They are also important because they come from a man who is both a doctor and a Communist. He told me there had always been friction between him and religion. His life completely changed in 1944, following a surreal event that overturned his mind.

He told me, "I had recently graduated. I was specializing in the clinic that Professor Cesare Frugoni supervised, but I wanted to earn some more money. That is why I saw patients at night around Rome. I was always in touch with a pharmacy that gave me the addresses where I had to go. I have to admit it was not easy to wake up in the middle of the night to go around the city.

Sometimes my wife, Luana, came with me, and when she was not available, there was my dog.

"One night, the pharmacy informed me that there was a phone call coming from Appia Nuova. I was in the car by myself, and it was difficult to drive because the weather was really bad; there were strong winds and rain. I was driving when I suddenly realized there was a bearded friar on the seat next to me. I opened my eyes wide, and I touched my face to wake up, but I was not sleeping. I was wide awake, and I was driving. That friar was familiar to me. Carlo Campanini, a famous actor and a dear friend of mine, had showed me many pictures of that friar. It was Padre Pio from Pietralcina. Campanini was one of his spiritual children, and he had often talked to me about him. But why was he in my car? I reached for him, but my fingers passed through his body, as if he were made of light.

"I had no time to think about what was happening because the friar started talking to me. Actually, he had no voice; he didn't make any sound. His thoughts simply entered my mind. He gave me information about the patient I was about to see. The patient was an old man who lived alone with his wife, and he had had a stroke. Padre Pio told me to avoid the practice of bloodletting, which was common at that time. He said I should instead use the medications I had in my bag. He knew exactly indeed what I was carrying in my case. This is what he told me, and then he disappeared.

"I kept driving. I was shocked, as if someone had hit me on my head. I was also very nervous. When I reached my destination, I found the old man that Padre Pio had described. His wife was desperately crying, and his condition was serious. I first thought about bloodletting, which was the most common practice, but I soon remembered Padre Pio's words. I took the medications in my bag and administered them. The old man began to recover. I stayed with them the whole night, and I left at sunrise. Before I left, I asked them if I could use their bathroom to wash my hands. While I was there, I heard the lady saying to her husband, 'This young doctor looks exactly like the one that Padre Pio told me about.' I quickly left the bathroom and asked her what she meant. The lady explained to me that she had had a dream about Padre Pio. He warned her that her husband was going to have a stroke, but she should not worry because a young doctor was going to take care of him. It was so amazing!

"I spent the following days thinking about what had happened. But above all, I kept thinking about that friar who had appeared next to me in the car. I knew he was Padre Pio, but I wanted to find out more. Why had he appeared? Why had he made me go to that old man's house? Maybe I would never get any answers, but going to San Giovanni Rotondo seemed like the only way to try.

"One night I was having dinner at Carlo Campanini's house. I pulled him aside, and I said, 'Carlo, you have to take me to Padre Pio; otherwise, I will go crazy.' I told him about my vision and the old sick man. That same night we drove to Gargano. We got there at four in the morning. There were already many people in line outside the monastery waiting for Mass. However, everybody recognized Campanini, and they let us into the monastery. We knocked on the door of Padre Pio's cell. He was getting ready for Mass. He came out, and when he saw me, he stared at me with his burning eyes. He said, 'Lazzarone! You finally came to visit me.' And he added, smiling, 'You know, Mario, you are not actually a talented doctor. You are talented because I am behind you, and I lead you!' It all made sense. I reexperienced that night, the vision of the friar in my car, the sick man, and his wife's dream. I was deeply touched. I fell on my knees, and I started crying. Padre Pio put a hand on my head, and from that moment, my life has changed forever.

"I have remained very close to him, and I visited him several times during his life. After his death, I became even closer to him. Here is an example. At the end of the 1980s, I was driving, and some friends of mine and my niece were in the car with me. I dangerously swerved on the asphalt. I lost control of the car, and it headed fast towards a precipice. If we had crashed down, we would have all died. But suddenly, a strong light, similar to the sun, appeared in front of us. The car stopped, and it headed back towards the road by itself, as if it were operated by remote control. The light vanished as quickly as it had appeared. I am sure it was Padre Pio's intercession, and nobody can change my mind."

6

"Nobody Wants to Carry the Cross."

In the previous story, Mario Spallone mentions Carlo Campanini, an actor who was one of Padre Pio's spiritual sons. Campanini's name is included in all the biographies on Padre Pio. Following his conversion, he became indeed one of the most fervent spiritual children of Padre Pio. His colleagues used to call him "Padre Pio's sacristan."

Campanini was born in 1906, and he was one of the most famous and beloved actors of the 1940s and 1950s. He died in 1984. My father knew him well, and he often told me about him. Campanini met Padre Pio in 1939. At that time, he worked as an actor in the theater, and he was often on tour away from home. It was hard because he was married and had three children. He was hoping to find a job that allowed him to be close to his children, but he only knew how to act. He was not a man of faith. When he was a child, he had attended the school *Fratelli delle Scuole Cristiane*. Every morning, before classes, the children had to attend Mass. This sort of imposition really bothered him, and for this reason, once he finished school, he no longer walked into a church.

Once in 1939, he was talking with Mario Amendola, a comedy writer. Campanini told him, "In the past, it was easier to believe in God. There were great saints, such as St. Francis, St. Anthony, or St. John Bosco. And they did miracles. Nowadays, saints no longer exist, and there are no miracles."

"That is not true," replied Amendola. "There is a friar in Apulia who does extraordinary things." And he told him what had happened to his cousin a few years before.

"He was jobless, and he was a volunteer in the Spanish War. When he came back, his wife told him, 'You are back because of Padre Pio. He prayed for you, and I promised him you would come and thank him.' My cousin then went to San Giovanni Rotondo, and he confided his concerns to Padre Pio. Padre Pio told him, 'Move to Falconara.' My cousin said, 'I can't. I have friends in Rome who help me once in a while. I would starve in Falconara.' But Padre Pio kept saying, 'Move to Falconara.' My cousin moved to that city with his wife and children. One morning, a man from Ancona was looking for him. He said, 'The federal sent me here. Tomorrow morning he will be waiting for you in his office.' My cousin showed up for the appointment. The federal asked him if he spoke Spanish. He said yes, and they immediately made him sign a contract. They offered him 100 lire a day, 3000 lire a month."

Campanini was impressed by the story. Once he was in Bari with his acting company. During his day off, he decided to go to San Giovanni Rotondo with Amendola. It was Thursday, and it was Holy Week. When they arrived at the monastery, they were hoping to see Padre Pio, but they were told he could not receive them. During Holy Week, Padre Pio's injuries were indeed more painful than during the rest of the year. This is why he could not receive anyone. Campanini and Amendola chose to stay near the monastery. They hoped to run into Padre Pio, even randomly.

While they were waiting, Campanini told jokes to everyone he came into contact with. Suddenly, a friar came out of the church. Campanini thought he looked like a giant. The friar asked them, "What do you want? You are not letting me pray." Campanini answered, "We are two humble artists." "We are all humble," Padre Pio replied. The two artists wanted to confess, so Padre Pio told them to come back the following morning.

Campanini confided what had happened in the confessional to my father. "Padre Pio did not let me talk; he knew everything about me. I promised him I would change my life, and he gave me absolution. I was not brave enough to ask him anything. However, I kept saying inside of me, 'Father, please, let me find a job near home. I will even work as a warehouseman, as long as I can live with my children.' I went back to Bari and then back to Rome. In Cinecittà they were about to start shooting *Addio giovinezza!* At that time, the Ministry of Culture assigned the roles. Four famous actors were nominated for the part of Leone: Nino Besozzi, a sort of Mastroianni of that time; Umberto Melnati, who worked with De Sica and was popular in the whole country; Paolo Stoppa; and Carlo Romano. I was not well-known in those circles, but for reasons I don't know, the role was eventually assigned to me. I went on to act in 106 additional movies, one after the other, and I became rich and famous. I was able to buy a house and live with my kids, as I had wished for. Padre Pio knew what I was hoping for in my heart."

This is the story that Campanini told my father. I went to Rome to visit Campanini's daughter, Maria Pia, in order to get some further details. She immediately explained to me that "Padre Pio was like a family member. We asked him for advice, and miracles actually happened in our lives. Following his fame, my dad somehow forgot Padre Pio. My father was in great demand. He was so famous. However, he led a somewhat libertine life, and he had affairs with different women. But at the same time, he felt a deep void. Once he told me he had everything, but it was like having an empty bag because his faith was missing.

"In 1950 he decided to go back to San Giovanni Rotondo. He confessed to Padre Pio, and they hugged each other. In that moment, my dad felt an intense tenderness. The next day, during Mass, he converted for good. He told us he had seen Padre Pio raising the goblet with difficulty, as if its weight was huge. A voice inside my father told him, 'Can you see that crown of thorns? You pressed it down, too, because of your sins. You also spit on Jesus' face.' My father was then really moved. He ran out of the church and burst into tears. From then on, he turned into a different person. He went to church every day. He always talked about Padre Pio, and some of his colleagues made fun of him. They nicknamed him 'Padre Pio's loudspeaker.' He turned down many movies, giving up a lot of money, because they were not suitable for children. But he was happy.

"I still keep a statue of Baby Jesus that used to be in front of Padre Pio's cell. He kissed it every time he was leaving the cell and every time he went in. One day, my dad asked him if he could have it, and Padre Pio gave it to him. My father went to San Giovanni Rotondo every time he could. He said he could not breathe when he was far away from Padre Pio. And soon the whole family traveled with him. That is why Padre Pio was like a family member for us. As I said, we were often helped by the grace of God, both when it came to big things and small daily ones. It showed us that Padre Pio was always with us.

"I remember, for example, that one day, my brother, who was studying architecture, was despairing because of an upcoming exam. 'I have no time to study. I have only studied a few topics: I will not get a good grade.' My father said, 'Well, let's send a telegram to Padre Pio and tell him about it.' The next day my brother took the exam. When he came back home, he was radiant: 'Dad, they just asked me questions about the few topics I had studied!'

"It was amazing to visit Padre Pio all together. He loved us, and he taught us so much, especially what it means to suffer. Once, my dad was with him in the hallway of the monastery, and there were so many people surrounding Padre Pio. They asked him to be healed or to solve one of their urgent problems. Later, when they were alone, Padre Pio told my father, 'You see, Carletto, all these people wish that their crosses were lifted. Nobody wants to carry the cross. But if they were really aware of the great value of suffering, they would carry their crosses every day.'

"When I was around Padre Pio, I was entranced and captivated by him. One day, during our stay in San Giovanni Rotondo, my mother asked me, laughing, 'Why do you always make that silly face when you look at Padre Pio?' 'Because I am too excited, and I can't control myself,' I said. A few hours later, I had an appointment with him. I walked into the monastery, and Padre Pio looked out the window. He smiled and shouted, 'Come here, silly face!' He knew exactly what my mother had told me.

"Both my daughters were healed miraculously. They owe so much to Padre Pio. My oldest daughter, Anna Grazia, was born in April 1968. She was in good health, but when she was five months old, she contracted a severe bowel disease. The doctors could not treat her, and we were heartbroken. She lost too much weight. She ate some special food that didn't seem to help. On September 23, I got a phone call, and I was informed that Padre Pio had died. I was devastated. I ran to my bedroom and fell on my knees and cried in front of his picture. I was overwhelmed by the loss and also crushed because my baby was dying. In that moment, my mother called me, shouting. I ran to her, and I realized that Anna Grazia's body had resumed its normal vital functions. She was completely healed. The doctors could not believe it, and in a short amount of time, she recovered as if nothing had happened.

"Years went by, and Monica was born in 1970. When she was eleven years old, she got caught in a door while she was playing. Her cheek was torn all the way up to the ear. I tried to fix it temporarily as I could, and then I took Monica quickly to the hospital. In the meantime, I kept telling myself, 'Padre Pio . . . Padre Pio . . . ' At the Santo Spirito hospital, I found Dr. Monti. He was well-known at that time because he had been able to fix the amputated arm of a worker who had had an accident. The doctor urgently gathered his team, they examined Monica, and they took her to the operating theater. I was terrified while I was waiting. I spoke to other doctors, and they told me that Dr. Monti never worked at the hospital in the morning, so they were surprised he was there on that day. The surgery went well. The following day the surgeons examined Monica, and they were stunned when they realized that her face was perfectly sensitive. It was amazing. Besides, I was told that her facial muscle was unharmed: it was like *someone* had moved it at the time of the accident. Inside of me, I obviously knew who that *someone* was.

"Afterward, we took Monica to San Giovanni Rotondo for plastic surgery. Dr. Melillo worked there, and he was a leader in his field. I remember I visited Padre Pio's grave and begged him to protect us: 'Please, send me a sign.' That night, Monica woke me up at three in the morning. She said, 'Mom, I dreamed about Padre Pio. I was with him, and dad was there, too. He stroked me, and he said, 'Melillo is a good doctor! Melillo is a good doctor!' That was the sign I was waiting for. It all worked out for the best."

7

"Come on! We Have to Do Our Duty!"

From 1964 until his death in 1968, Padre Pio was flanked by a priest, as his superior suggested. He helped him during Mass and when he had to change vestments. He went to church with Padre Pio and to the dining hall. When Padre Pio's health got worse, he stopped eating in the dining hall with his brothers, so the priest brought him his meals to his room. This priest's name was Fr. Silvano from Cerignola.

His name, however, is rarely mentioned in Padre Pio's biographies or in the stories of those who knew him because Fr. Silvano is no longer a priest. Following Padre Pio's death, he left the Franciscans, the Pope dispensed him from his vows, and he got married and started a family. He basically disappeared from Padre Pio's entourage. After some diligent research, I was able to locate him, and I visited him in Ascoli Piceno. Fr. Silvano is now Michele Monopoli. He is eighty-eight years old, he has been widowed since 2001, and he has a son. I have never seen eyes as bright as his and a smile as excited as his when he talks about Padre Pio. There were tears in his eyes. Michele has so many stories, descriptions, and details to share about Padre

Pio's daily life. Listening to him was an honor and an amazing opportunity.

He told me, "When I was around Padre Pio, I foretasted heaven. He was a saint. I felt like one of God's favorites because I was lucky to spend time with him. I helped him early in the morning during the Mass. And I was there for him throughout the day. I took him to his room, or I helped him while he was in the confessional. When we were walking together, he often leaned on my arm and smiled. Those moments were peaceful and immensely joyful. I feel I am still one of his brothers, that I am still a friar. I pray every day, and I always feel Padre Pio's presence close to me. I am old, I know I do not have much time left. I gaze at the trails left behind by the airplanes in the sky, and I think about the moment my soul will fly to heaven. Padre Pio will be waiting for me and for his followers, as he promised.

"I was sent to the monastery in San Giovanni Rotondo in 1964. My duties were to take care of the church and to help Padre Pio. He celebrated only one Mass a day, at five in the morning. His day always started very early. He did not sleep much, and he was already up at two. I picked him up in his room and he used to say, 'Son, I have been up since two. I meditated, and now I am ready for the Mass.' Then, I took him to the sacristy and helped him get dressed. Padre Pio used to take his gloves off and give them to me. They were hiding his stigmata. I then put them in the tunic. I remember their intense strawberry scent. When he was not wearing his gloves, Padre Pio's sores were very visible. I did not stare at them too much because I knew he did not appreciate it. But you could actually see the holes on his palms.

"For Padre Pio, the most beautiful and important moment was being at the altar. He was really focused during Mass, absorbed in his prayers. His face was first joyful, and then pale, as if he had lost all his strength. When he was at the altar, Padre Pio actually reexperienced Christ's Passion: it was mystical. I was close to him, and I helped him with the reading of the missal. My forefinger was scrolling on the lines so that he would not make mistakes. After Mass, the church was crowded with people that wanted to talk to him or give him letters. He tried to pay attention to all of them. Then, he rested for an hour, then drank an herbal infusion and, sometimes, some milk. At 6:30 he was ready to hear confessions. Padre Pio was seventy-eight years old, he was sick, and he had been having stigmata for fifty years. But he never stopped. He was mainly concerned about the people that needed him. The confessional was his goal. He used to tell me, 'Come on! We have to do our duty! Let's go to work!' And he quickened his pace even if it was painful.

"When he heard confessions, a priest had to be next to him. Padre Pio was indeed partially deaf, and he talked loudly in the confessional. You could hear everything, so his assistant, which was I, had to be a priest because he listened to the penitents' sins. Padre Pio was as sweet as a father with them, but sometimes he was also harsh and inflexible. He did not tolerate the people that did not go to church on Sunday or who were unfaithful. Once in a while, I could hear him saying, 'Have you given your soul to the devil? Don't you know that Sunday is God's day?' or 'Go make up with your wife, and then you will be forgiven!'

"I remember that on January 30, 1965, the Inter soccer team came to San Giovanni Rotondo to meet Padre Pio. There were Helenio Herrera, who was the coach, Sandro Mazzola, Giacinto Facchetti, Mario Corso, Armando Picchi, Liz Suarez, and some of the team managers. The next day they were going to play against Foggia, which was playing for the first time in the Premier League. That day, around six in the morning, I was helping Padre Pio with confessions. Then Mazzola and Picchi approached me. They were intimidated, and they asked me if they could confess to Padre Pio. However, people were supposed to book in advance, and their names were not on the list. I told them they had to wait. But Mazzola said, 'We are here without our coach's authorization, and there could be disciplinary measures. Please, let us meet Padre Pio. We can't go back home if we don't talk to him.' In that moment, I heard Padre Pio's voice, saying, 'Send me another one!' So I brought Mazzola into the confessional, jumping the line. Again, after a while, 'Send me another one.' And it was Picchi's turn. Later, I saw them leaving the monastery: they were touched.

"So many memories! Another one comes to my mind. It was Ash Wednesday 1965. Padre Pio had not received ashes in the morning because he was busy in the confessional. In the afternoon, he asked me, 'Who is going to scatter the ashes on my head?' I replied that his superior could likely do it by the end of the day. He said, 'Do I need to wait until tonight? Now, now! You can do it!' He took his stole off, and he let me wear it. Then he lowered his head, waiting for the ashes. It was unforgettable.

"When I was young, I had a beautiful voice. While I was a theology student, I was also a solo tenor at the *Schola Cantorum* in Campobasso. Sometimes I sang in San Giovanni Rotondo as well. One day, I started singing the song 'Mamma' because I knew Padre Pio really liked it. He asked, 'Who is singing?' My brothers pointed at me. And Padre Pio said, 'Oh, it was *sto cacchiato,*' which in dialect means 'young man.' And he added, 'Your voice touched me even more than that of Beniamino Gigli!'

"After his death, things changed. I think I was already going through a personal crisis. I really wanted to have a baby and become a dad. I wondered if I could serve God even if I left the monastery. I discussed this with one of my superiors, a very wise man. He told me, 'It is better to be a good layman rather than a bad priest.' I received dispensation from my vows, thanks to Pope Paul VI. I went to work for a butcher shop in Bevazzana, in the province of Udine. I met a girl there, we got married, and we started our family. But I never stopped thinking about Padre Pio and the moments we shared in the monastery. We talked about everything, and he always asked me many questions. He used to worry about the weather forecast because he feared that the rain or the snow would affect people's journey to visit him. That is how he was: he never stopped worrying about his followers. I know he is waiting to hug me in heaven."

8

His Eyes Pierced Your Soul

As Michele Monopoli, formerly Fr. Silvano, said, The Inter soccer team visited Padre Pio in January 1965. The team's coach was Helenio Herrera. It was an interesting event. But what is even more interesting is player Sandro Mazzola's secret visit to the monastery on the morning of the match. I wanted to find out more, so I went to Mazzola's house in Monza. I found out that his devotion began during his childhood.

He said, "When I was a child, I prayed to Padre Pio. I asked him to let me become a soccer player, as good as my father. He listened to me because that is exactly what happened. I ended up playing for Helenio Herrera's Inter in the Premier League. It was the best team in the 1960s. I played for the national team, I took part in the most important matches, and I won prestigious awards. I wanted to thank Padre Pio for everything, so in January 1965, I visited him."

Sandro Mazzola is a soccer celebrity. He is believed to be one of the all-time most talented Italian soccer players. He excited a whole generation of fans, like his father, Valentino Mazzola, who was the great striker of the Turin team. Valentino died in 1949 in the Superga air crash. It took me time to find Mazzola's phone number, but thanks to some of my friends who are journalists, I was eventually able to talk to him. I explained to him who I was and what I did, and his answer was, "Am I supposed to tell you about Padre Pio? Of course!"

I am an Inter soccer fan. It is therefore difficult to describe how excited I was to meet Mazzola. I wondered if he had met Padre Pio, not simply because the whole team went to San Giovanni, but for a more personal reason, and Mazzola immediately confirmed that. "I told him about my father. I told him I missed him, and I played soccer in order to feel him next to me. I also told him about another topic that I held very dear. I will never forget how I felt when I was in front of him. When I think about it, even now, I am breathless.

"Padre Pio was like a family member. But let's start from the beginning. Following my father's death, we moved to Cassano d'Adda, the village where my father was born. My mother worked, so my grandmother and my aunt took care of me and my brother, Ferruccio. They were really devoted to Padre Pio. Every night, they told us amazing stories about him. I still remember it; we all slept in a big room. My brother and I shared the same bed. My grandmother, my aunt, and my great-grandparents were also there. Before falling asleep, we listened to a story about Padre Pio. They told us about his miracles and wonders, his stigmata, and his cures. They also told us he could see into people's hearts. My grandma and my aunt had never met him personally, but they were telling us what they had read or what the priest at church had said. I believe that they sometimes exaggerated, not because they wanted to impress us, but rather because of their strong faith. I was seven years old, and those magical stories fascinated me. I envisioned Padre Pio as an old, kind, and wise man. I also thought of him as a distant relative, someone I had never seen but whose presence could be perceived.

"When I was fifteen years old, I joined the youth team of Inter. When I started playing soccer, people would say, 'What does he think he is doing? He will never be like his father!' Those comments hurt me. I did not wish to compete with my father. I simply liked soccer, and when I played, I felt closer to my dad. But the criticisms hurt me, so I used to go to church and pray to Padre Pio. I said, 'Let me become a soccer player as good as my father. I do not care if I die as young as him; let me be talented.' I just wanted to be like my dad, who had left me so soon. Those were the prayers of a kid with a heart full of dreams. And Padre Pio really loved dreams.

"One day, when I confessed to my priest, I told him about my prayers. He refused to forgive me. He said that when I said would die young as long as I could play soccer, I committed a severe sin. That was not what I had wished for. I was just a kid, and the priest's words impressed me. I felt guilty for many years, until 1965, when I finally met Padre Pio in person.

"But let's go in order. Time went by, and I realized I kept improving. It looked like Padre Pio had listened to my prayers. And I told myself, 'If I committed a mortal sin, why is my dream coming true?' My faith and my trust in Padre Pio clashed with the words of that priest, and I could not come to terms with it. I was very confused. Padre Pio was the only one who could help me understand, so when I had the chance to go to San Giovanni Rotondo, I took advantage of it.

"I had been playing for Inter for four years. It was the championship of 1964/1965. That year, the Foggia team was playing for the first time in the Premier League. We had already played them in September in San Siro, and we had won. The next match was scheduled on Sunday, January 31, 1965. The day before, our coach, Helenio Herrera, decided to take the whole team to San Giovanni Rotondo. It is 40 kilometers (25 miles) away from Foggia. I think he wanted to ask Padre Pio to let us win. His proposal was welcomed among the players since several players had heard about Padre Pio, and they were excited to meet him. A few of us wanted to talk to him about something important to us. In my case, it was my father. Armando Picchi hoped to get news about his brother who had been missing since the war. I think Giorgio Dellagiovanna wanted to find out about his mother because he had never met her.

"On that day, Saturday, January 30, 1965, Padre Pio was sitting with his brothers. We, members of the team, were basically occupying the whole hallway that led to the small living room where he used to receive guests. When they told him that the Inter team had come to visit him, he said, 'Why are they here? They are going to lose against Foggia anyway. But they will win the championship.' We lost 3-2. It was a memorable match. But as Padre Pio predicted, we won the championship, with a 3-point win over Milan.

"Among all those people, I did not have a chance to talk to Padre Pio alone as I wished. I obviously could not go back to Milan without doing it. When was I going to get another opportunity? I then asked a friar how I could get a private encounter with Padre Pio. He told me to come back the following day at five in the morning. I could see him after Mass, when he would begin hearing confessions. But it was the day of the match! That meant I had to leave the hotel secretly. If Herrera had found out about it, he would have not have allowed me to play. At that time, they could even decide not to pay you for such behavior! Herrera was very strict. I chose to run the risk, and I made arrangements with two of my teammates, Picchi and Dellagiovanna. We were as quiet as mice: before sunrise we left our hotel in Foggia, and we got to the monastery in San Giovanni Rotondo. Even though it was early, there were many people waiting to enter the church. I remember that everybody was singing, and there was a peaceful climate. After Mass, the friar I had spoken to the previous day took us to Padre Pio. We jumped the entire queue. When I ended up in front of him, I was speechless.

"My legs were shaking. I had grown up hearing about him, and now he was there: it felt impossible. His eyes pierced your soul, but I was not intimidated. I felt like I was finally with a father that I had not seen in a long time. I told him about me, about my dad's death. I also mentioned my childhood prayers to him, how I had been feeling guilty because I was told I had committed a sin. Padre Pio started laughing. It was nice to watch him laughing; my soul was relieved. He blessed me, and he gave me absolution. Three Our Fathers, Hail Marys, Glory Be's were my penance. My heart was overjoyed. I stayed in the church, waiting for my two teammates who were talking to Padre Pio, and then we went back to the hotel. We went to bed. I am sure the coach was aware of our escape, but he never said anything. Perhaps he knew we were going to visit Padre Pio, and he was happy about it.

"This is what happened. After that, I have never stopped turning to Padre Pio during my prayers. I am fond of him. It felt like he was the father that I did not have the chance to meet."

9

Butterflies and Little Birds

Aurelio Fierro died in 2005, at the age of eighty-two. He was a star of Neapolitan music. Before his death, I was able to meet him and ask him about Padre Pio, whom he knew very well. "I was a friend of his, and I could spend time with him privately, when he was away from the crowd," Fierro said. "I can assure you that it was great to be with him. Padre Pio also helped me to win the *Festival della Canzone Napoletana*, and he saved my life during a scary car accident in Brazil."

Aurelio Fierro was a successful, wealthy, and confident man. He took part in six Sanremo Music Festivals. He was the winner of five *Festival della Canzone Napoletana* and of one *Canzonissima*. He was an actor, and he played with artists such as Tina Pica, Pupella Maggio, Nino Manfredi, and Sylva Koscina. He was also a producer, writer, politician, and owner of two restaurants in Naples, always full of customers. But when he talked about Padre Pio, he got excited like a child, and his eyes clouded with tears.

"When I was close to him, I was happy. He released an energy that gave me strength and well-being. I often visited him. I was a familiar face to the friars of the monastery in San Giovanni Rotondo. They used to let me in and take me immediately to Padre Pio. In the evening, I walked with him in the vegetable garden, and that was the best moment. In the garden, we were in nature. We were surrounded by fireflies, crickets, the sounds of dusk, and the stars that were starting to show up in the sky. Padre Pio was radiant with joy. He kept looking around, like an amazed child. Everything excited him: a flying butterfly, the song of a small bird, the color of the flowers or of the sunset. He took me by the arm, and said, 'Do you see how beautiful it is?'

"I met him in 1958. I was supposed to take part in the *Festival della Canzone Napoletana*, which I had already won two years before. It was an important event, very popular, that was even broadcast in Europe. However, that year I got sick. I thought it was just the flu, but a couple of days before the show, my temperature got higher, around 40 degrees Celsius (104 Fahrenheit). The doctor said it was bronchial pneumonia. There was no way I could sing on stage—or win! My father, Raffaele, was very devoted to Padre Pio, so he decided to go to San Giovanni Rotondo to ask him to pray for me. My dad knew how important the festival was for my career, and the first thing that came to his mind was to turn to Padre Pio. All the followers did the same. My sister informed me, telling me that our father was on his way to Gargano. I smiled, and I felt affection for him. Of course, I did not say anything to him: I did not want to hurt his feelings and his faith. But I considered his decision to be that of an old naive man. I was familiar with Padre Pio's fame, what people said about him. I knew my parents were devoted to him, but I was skeptical. In my opinion, the wonders that people talked about were exaggerations, similar to tales to make children fall asleep.

"The day of the show, I decided to perform anyway. I was crazy, because I was very sick, and it was risky. But I did not want to disappoint my fans. Besides, it was a prestigious event. Some of the contestants were Nunzio Gallo, Giacomo Rondinella, Nino Taranto, and Marisa Del Frate. It would have been a shame to not be among them. Therefore, I did not follow my doctor's advice, I took a lot of medicine, and I went on stage. I felt really bad: I had mucus, sore throat, and a cough. When it was my turn, I was shaking. The music started, I trusted in Virgin Mary, and I began singing. It was amazing: my voice was clear and strong. I was singing, and at the same time, I was thinking, 'What is going on?' My voice was perfectly fine; it was not the voice of a person with bronchial pneumonia. It looked like the voice was coming from the throat of a healthy singer. The performance was a success, and the judges later declared me the winner.

"The next day, while I was checking the mail, I found a postcard from my father. He had sent it four days before from San Giovanni Rotondo. It said, 'I talked to Padre Pio, and he told me not to worry because you will win!' I could not believe it. How could this friar already know I was going to win, four days before the show? Was he the one who had actually helped me, like my father had asked him? In that case, I had no time to waste. I had to meet this friar in person, and I had to thank him.

"A few weeks later, I had the opportunity to do it. I was on a tour in Apulia, and I went to San Giovanni Rotondo. On my way there, there was a severe storm: thunder, lightning, and thick rain that did not allow me to see anything. But as I approached the village, the weather improved, and when I arrived at the monastery, the sun was shining. The friars recognized me immediately because they had seen my picture in the newspapers. I asked them if I could meet Padre Pio, and they introduced me to him. He was in the vegetable garden. The friars, all excited, told him, 'This is Aurelio Fierro, the famous singer.' He smiled, 'I know, I know.' And then, looking at me, he added, 'You are finally here. What a beautiful day you brought! Yesterday it rained, and now there is a beautiful sun.'

"Padre Pio fascinated me. I became his friend, and I often visited him. In 1961, I visited him before leaving for an important tour in Brazil. He put a hand on my head, he closed his eyes, and he was silent for a while. Then he blessed me, saying, 'Do not worry, son; I am with you.' I did not understand immediately the meaning of his sentence, but I did later. The trip was quiet. A friend of mine picked me up with a very big American car at the airport of San Paolo. During the journey, while we were descending a curvy mountain road, my friend, who was driving, shouted, 'The car does not slow down! The brakes are broken!' The car was accelerating. On one side of the road, there was a ravine, while on the other side, there was a mountain. If we had crashed into the rocky side, the car would have overturned and bounced, and it would have fallen into the ravine. There was no way out. I desperately thought about Padre Pio. I grabbed the rosary that he had given me and that I kept in my pocket. Suddenly, I heard a loud bang. I was catapulted from the back seat against the windshield. I tried to move: I was alive. My friend was unhurt, too. The car had crashed into the side of the mountain, but inexplicably, it was not a rocky wall, but rather a sandy one. The violent impact was cushioned, and neither of us was injured. I was squeezing the rosary in my hands, and I thought, 'Padre Pio saved me.'

"When I was back in Italy, I went straight to San Giovanni Rotondo to thank him in person. When he saw me, before I could even speak, he said, smiling, 'I told you to not be afraid because I was going to be there with you.' So I hugged him, crying."

10

It Was Impossible Not to Fall in Love with Him

"Padre Pio was a lighthouse for all of us. It was common in the village to go to him to get his blessing or his advice. The mothers, for example, took their babies or their kids that were going to receive Holy Communion to Padre Pio. They did not take them to the monastery of the Capuchin monks. They asked for a special blessing. That was how I met him."

This is what Professor Biagio Russo, who is seventy-five years old, told me. He is now retired, but he was a math and science teacher in middle school. He is currently a poet and a writer, and he met Padre Pio when he was a child. "Padre Pio was a *sangiuuannare* like us," Russo said, using a dialectal term that means "a citizen of San Giovanni Rotondo." "He was clearly very attached to his native town, and he got emotional when somebody from Pietralcina visited him. But at the same time, he really loved our village and its people, who had protected him on many occasions. He considered himself a *sangiuuannare*, and before his death, he wrote a letter to the mayor, Francesco Morcaldi, asking to be buried in San Giovanni.

"As I said, it was common to take newborns to Padre Pio. It is likely that my mother attended his Mass, holding me in her arms. However, I met him for the first time in person in 1953, during the time of my First Communion. I had already received it in the parish of my village, but after that, I went straight to the monastery of the friars to get Padre Pio's blessing and for him to hear my confession. It was sort of a tradition. It was like getting a seal, so people wanted to be blessed by him, who was believed to be a saint. Padre Pio's confessional was made of a two-sided prie-dieu and of a thick metal grill, which separated the priest from the penitent. But when children confessed to him, it was face-to-face. He used to open the curtain, and we used to bow to him, with our hands on his knees. It felt like talking to a caring grandfather rather than giving a confession. But he could also be a strict grandfather.

"I have never forgotten one event. I think I was ten years old, and I went to the cinema to watch a movie about ancient Romans. There were war scenes, but they were not improper. I decided to mention it to Padre Pio anyway. I told him, 'I watched a movie, but I did not find it sinful.' His eyes were on fire. He shouted, 'Go away! First you confess, and then you prove your innocence; go away!' I was so ashamed. But it was a valuable lesson. I understood that confession is not a game. You rely on God's mercy, and there is no need to excuse yourself for your behavior. I never forgot it.

"During those years, I often attended Padre Pio's Mass. I remember some people complaining because the celebration was too long. It could last three hours. It is true, three hours are long. But we can't forget that Padre Pio, at the altar, interceded for all the faithful's requests before God—all of them, both written and oral—and he did not forget a single one. The requests were countless. Padre Pio was meticulous; he did not want to forget about anyone, so he disclosed every single request to God. This also explains why he needed much time.

"When I was a young man, I joined 'Gifra,' *Gioventù Francescana*, Franciscan Youth. One of our tasks was to play songs for the Sunday Mass at 9:30 a.m. in the monastery. Padre Pio's Mass took place at five in the morning, and it was mainly attended by adults. The one at 9:30 was more popular among young people, but he attended it anyway. He sat in the choir, near the crucifix in front of which he had gotten the stigmata in 1918. He followed Mass from up there, praying. He watched us, and sometimes he smiled. It was impossible not to fall in love with Padre Pio. He has been in my heart for all my life. He watched over my family, and once, he made me realize he was close to us.

"My daughter Anna wanted to become a journalist and a biologist. She enrolled at the University of Ferrara, and during her time there, she lived with the Carmelite nuns. She came home just before the summer. She told us she was not going to come on vacation with us because she had to go to Lisieux, in Normandy, to visit St. Thérèse of Lisieux's house. She was inflexible, and she left: I was very worried. I could not understand, and I was concerned about her, her studies, and her future. But every night, when I went to bed, an amazing scent of roses enveloped me. There were no flowers in the house, but the scent was intense. I am sure it was Padre Pio's caress. He was telling me to stay calm, because he was watching over my daughter. Anna became a nun, and now she is Sr. Therese of Jesus. She is the prioress of the Carmelite monastery in Parma.

"Even my Uncle Nicola became a monk because of Padre Pio. He was a carpenter, but in 1951 he decided to move to Australia to seek his fortune. Before leaving, he wanted to say goodbye to Padre Pio, so he went to the monastery, and he found him in the confessional. Padre Pio opened the curtain, came out of the confessional, and moved to the sacristy. My Uncle Nicola followed him and noticed he was waiting for him. Padre Pio smiled at him, and he held out his hand to my uncle so that he could kiss it. Then Padre Pio blessed him. The journey by ship to Australia was very long. Once he got there, my uncle could not get off the ship because he had a very high temperature. He was really sick, and it almost seemed that something was preventing him from disembarking. One night he dreamed about Padre Pio. He saw him carrying the cross on his shoulders, and the cross was digging in the soil, leaving a furrow. When my uncle woke up, he had completely recovered. But he was also a different person. Two years later, he became a Capuchin monk named Fr. Antonio. For several years, he worked as a missionary in Australia, and when he came back to Italy, Padre Pio had already died. Nevertheless, he lived in the monastery of San Giovanni Rotondo, and he was also the chaplain of *Casa Sollievo della Sofferenza*. He died in 1991. My uncle always talked about Padre Pio, his loving gaze, and how he was able to read people's hearts."

11

Little Presents in the Pockets

Mrs. Grazia Pia Grifa attended the monastery every day when she was a child. She also told me that children confessed to Padre Pio, who was loving and caring like a grandfather. She said, "I grew up with Padre Pio. We went to the monastery, and I saw him every day. I was in the church choir, and he was often present at our rehearsals. He liked to sing with us, and he was extremely tender. When we confessed to him, Padre Pio did not make us walk into the confessional, so there was no grating between us. I could look at him closely: his eyes were profound and sweet. Then I always asked him for a keepsake. He used to look for it in his pocket and then give it to me."

Mrs. Grazia Pia was born in San Giovanni Rotondo in 1944. Now she lives in Taranto, where her husband, the well-known sculptor Michele Miglionico, has his studio. "Padre Pio knew me even before I was born. My mother already had three sons, so she really wanted a daughter. But she could not get pregnant. She told Padre Pio about her desire. He said, 'Go, and do not worry. Pray to *Madonna delle Grazie*, and she will listen to you.' A month later, my mom found out she was pregnant. When I was born, I was named after both *Madonna delle*

Grazie and Padre Pio, to thank them. This is why my name is Grazia Pia.

"When I was a child, I went to the monastery every day. I went there with my friends for Mass, the choir, or catechism. I confessed to Padre Pio for the first time, and then I received my First Communion. The confessional was only for adults. He listened to children while he was sitting on a chair in the church. On those occasions, when you were very close to him, you could look into his eyes. I remember they were dark and profound. And I remember the intense scent that surrounded him, especially when I kissed his hand. Every time, after the absolution, I asked him for a present. 'Father, can I have a keepsake?' He smiled, he put his hand in the front pocket of his tunic, and he always had something for me: the picture of a saint, a rosary, a small medal with the picture of the Virgin Mary, or candy. Once, around Christmas, he gave me a little statue of Baby Jesus. I have kept all those objects. I still keep them because those are the gifts of a saint.

"As I said, I was a member of the choir at Padre Pio's Mass. He often came to sing with us during the rehearsals. His favorite song was "*Gesù Cristo Peccirillo,*" a Neapolitan song by Sant'Alfonso Maria de' Liguori. He listened to it, and he got emotional. There were tears in his eyes.

"At the end of Mass, there were always many people waiting to kiss his hand and to be blessed. He could not therefore pay attention to the children. We were not able to say goodbye to him if we did not elbow our way in. Once, at Christmas, after Mass, I went to the sacristy with everybody else, for the season's greetings. There was a large crowd, and I felt like everyone but me was kissing Padre Pio's hand. I was annoyed, so I shouted, 'What about me?' He looked at me: I was tiny, and the people were squashing me. He smiled, and he stretched out his hand.

'There you go!' he said. I felt special because he had noticed me. But you always felt special when you were with him. It was like experiencing heaven in advance.

"I remember that one day I was wearing a toy watch. It was made of cardboard, the hours had been written with a pencil, and it was tied around my wrist with a rubber band. Padre Pio stared at it and smiled. He asked me, 'What time is it?' 'No, Father, it is fake.' And he said, 'Does this watch work or not?' He kindly made fun of us. He joked with all the children. He loved spending time with them and making them laugh.

"On a different occasion, he spread out a big blue handkerchief on his knees, and he took a little metal box out of his pocket. He kept snuff in it. Sometimes Padre Pio liked to take snuff, or *pizzicare*, as they used to say. But I had never seen him doing it. When I saw the contents of the box, I asked him, 'Father, is it cocoa?' He laughed. 'Do not be silly! It is tobacco. I use it to sneeze; it helps my breathing.'

"He really liked the scent of verbena, which is also called *erba luigia* or *cedrina*. He liked to keep some of its leaves in the confessional, and sometimes he smelled them. The lady who supervised the choir grew verbena in her garden. One day, I took some of it to Padre Pio. He was pleased, and he asked me, laughing, 'Are you a shop owner now?'

I also remember that Padre Pio really cared about decorum when it came to clothing. Girls were always supposed to wear a long dress and a handkerchief on the head. One day, when I was sixteen years old, I wanted to go to confession. My skirt was slightly above the knees. He said, 'Go lengthen your skirt!' Fr. Pellegrino, one of his brothers, was nearby. He gave me a long raincoat. I went back to the confessional wearing it, but I did not deceive Padre Pio. He laughed, 'Is it a carnival costume? Come back only when your skirt is longer.'

"When I grew up, I used to ask him for advice about boys. One day, I asked him about a specific boy who was courting me. I had not even finished asking my question when he said, seriously, 'No! You need to send him away! Otherwise, next time, I will send you away!' He showed me then that he knew everything. However, his harsh comment intimidated me, and it also made me a little angry. But it did not last long. I quickly realized that Padre Pio always knew what was best for his spiritual children, so I could trust him. I was worried when I fell in love with Michele, who later became my husband. I thought, 'What if I am told he is not good for me?' I did not have the courage to talk to Padre Pio because I was too afraid he would have told me again that he was not the man for me. At the same time, I wanted to hear his opinion. So I sent one of his brothers to ask him if I could accept Michele's attentions. Padre Pio answered, 'Yes, she can!' I heaved a sigh of relief; I was happy."

12

Violets and Incense Scent

The first time I heard about Padre Pio's love for snuff was in 1999, when I met Fr. Michelangelo Bazzali. Fr. Michelangelo died the following year at the age of ninety-one. I remember with excitement our encounter in his study in the monastery of Scandiano, in the province of Reggio Emilia. The room was packed with books all the way up to the ceiling. Fr. Michelangelo was well-known among the Capuchin monks. He was a writer, an esteemed poet, and a famous preacher. He was asked to be in charge of leading the Spiritual Exercises by the entourage of Pope Pio XII. He had also been one of Padre Pio's brothers in San Giovanni Rotondo for twenty-five years. He could talk about Padre Pio's daily and private life, such as his passion for snuff, which made me curious because this facet of Padre Pio made him seem more earthly. Fr. Michelangelo told me, "Yes, he was a great saint, but in everyday life, he was a regular, loving, and funny person. He liked joking, eating pasta, drinking a beer stein in the summer, and taking snuff sometimes.

"Living with Padre Pio was beautiful and unforgettable. It was a great period of my life. I saw him every day, and we were really close friends. We lived all together in the monastery, so I did not merely see him during Mass or when he was praying in the church. I was with him also at lunch and dinner, in the evening, and during the breaks in the monastery.

"I met him in 1945. He was an amazing brother, funny and lively. He was always happy and ready to joke; he loved telling funny stories. He lived his holiness privately. With the exception of his hands with the stigmata, on the outside he looked like a friendly and jolly friar. I used to sit next to him in the dining hall. He did not eat much. He usually tried the food, and then he gave it to some of his brothers who were hungrier. He never had breakfast or dinner. In the evening, he often did not come to the dining hall, and he asked the superior if he could stay in the church, praying. He had some pasta or some seafood for lunch, with a big glass of wine. In the afternoon, especially in the summer, he loved drinking a cold beer. During Lent, or on the eves of the celebrations dedicated to the Virgin Mary, he made small sacrifices. He gave up wine, beer, and even lunch, so he ended up fasting the whole day.

"Padre Pio loved taking snuff, in moderation. It helped him breathe better because he suffered from sinusitis. He used the *Sant'Antonino* tobacco, which came from Sicily. Dr. Mario Sanvico was one of his collaborators at *Casa Sollievo della Sofferenza*. One night, Padre Pio was about to take snuff, when the doctor said, joking, 'He could not become a saint because he took snuff!' Padre Pio stopped for a while, with his hand in the air. He answered, 'I do not want to inconvenience anyone,' and he moved the tobacco closer to his nose.

"He did not sleep much. He went back to his cell around nine in the evening, but he did not fall asleep immediately. He was awake, praying. Nobody knew exactly what he did at night. Apparently, he was capable of bilocation, so he went around the world to help the people that asked for his help. He celebrated

Mass at five in the morning, but he woke up before three o'clock to pray and meditate. Ten minutes before Mass, I went to his cell to call him, and he was always ready.

"When you were next to Padre Pio, you always smelled a beautiful and delicate scent. Its origin was unknown. It kept happening since 1918, when Padre Pio got the stigmata. Somebody maliciously claimed that he used expensive fragrances, but it is not true. The fact that it could be smelled even from kilometers away proves it. Actually, it was a sort of message. Padre Pio indeed used the scent to let us perceive his presence. He kept doing the same after his death: there is evidence of it. It is, however, difficult to describe that fragrance because it was never the same. Padre Pio emanated different scents according to the circumstances. A pansies fragrance, for example, meant humility; the incense scent was an invitation to prayer; the scent of roses meant that a favor was on the way; the lavender scent referred to domestic harmony; the scent of camphor meant suffering, while the carnation scent meant protection.

"Living with Padre Pio meant witnessing unbelievable and absurd episodes that logic could not explain. I witnessed many of them. I especially remember one of them because it concerned me. One day, Padre Pio gave me his tunic. His superiors did not allow him to give his personal belongings away, and Padre Pio followed the rules scrupulously. But sometimes he made an exception. He knew I really wanted something that belonged to him. That is why, when I was about to leave the monastery for a long time to preach, he said to me, 'Wait a moment. I have to give you my tunic.' He went to his cell, he grabbed the old tunic, and he hid it, using some newspapers, so that the other friars could not see it. He furtively gave it to me, saying, 'Be careful; hide it.' I hid it in my suitcase. I left with a few people that were taking me to Foggia by car. There was a big storm during the journey, with heavy rain and wind. The road was flooded, and it had become dangerous. The driver lost control of the car, which began skidding as if it were on ice. Then the car started spinning around, moving closer to the roadside and to the ravine that was below. But we did not fall. We were shocked because we were sure we were going to crash. However, the car suddenly stopped. It was immobilized as if it had been anchored. And the suitcase where I was keeping Padre Pio's tunic emanated a delicate scent of flowers that filled the car. Padre Pio had saved us."

13

"God Give You Back a Hundred; a Thousand Doubles for One."

"Padre Pio led my life, but I found it out later. When I was a young doctor, I saw him every day, but I did not grasp his holiness or his charisma. Anyway, Padre Pio was there, and he helped me and protected me like a caring parent."

These are the words of Professor Graziano Pretto. He is a professor at the Catholic University in Rome. He was the head physician of the ear-nose-throat department at *Casa Sollievo della Sofferenza*, the hospital founded by Padre Pio in 1956. Padre Pio was the one who wanted him in his hospital. "I did not agree. But Padre Pio knew everything about me, and he already knew I would never leave San Giovanni Rotondo."

"It was in the mid-1960s. I was the assistant of the famous Professor Michele Arslan, the head physician of the university clinic in Padoa. Professor Arslan had visited Padre Pio, who explicitly asked him to send somebody from his clinic to *Casa Sollievo*, in order to open an ear-nose-throat department. But nobody was willing to accept that job. It was understandable because at that time, San Giovanni Rotondo looked like a desert. There was nothing. Moving there to open a ward was risky. It meant starting from scratch, and nobody wanted to undertake that adventure.

"One day, I also visited Padre Pio, together with two friends. I was not a believer; I was simply curious. I had read about him in the newspapers, and I wanted to meet in person the friar who worked wonders. Two aspects of that visit impressed me. As soon as I walked into the monastery, an intense flower scent enveloped me. And then it was Padre Pio's gaze, so profound I felt like it was passing through me. However, we did not actually click—at least that was what I thought.

"In the meantime, nobody among the doctors was available to move to *Casa Sollievo*. Arslan asked me to do it. 'Just for six months,' he said. I was the last assistant to join his team, so I could not refuse. Reluctantly, I accepted and I left. It was July 1, 1966.

"Three days after my arrival, I was told that Padre Pio wanted me to examine him. I have to admit I was not impressed because, as I said, I was not a believer. Actually, to be honest, all those people that kneeled down in front of Padre Pio annoyed me. I thought, 'He's just a priest; he's not a saint!' Anyway, he had asked for me, so I went to him. I found him sitting on the porch. When I moved closer to him, he abruptly said, 'Be careful with my feet!' His tone surprised me, and it also bothered me. I thought, 'Why does he ask for me if the first thing he tells me is to keep off his feet? How rude!' I could not imagine that his feet were injured and that more than one person had likely touched them clumsily, causing him pain.

"That day, I examined him. Padre Pio could only partially hear. It was difficult in the confessional because the penitents had to shout. We opted for some insufflations that I would give him myself. That is how I started to spend time with him, but we did not talk much. I used to go to the porch where he was waiting for me, and I asked him how he felt. He always answered, 'I feel as God wishes.' I proceeded to do the insufflation, and in the end, he used to say, '*Dio ti renda cento, mille doppie per una*' (God give you back a hundred; a thousand doubles for one). At first, I did not understand what it meant, but then I found out it was the special blessing he used to wish me the best.

"One day, I was among those people waiting for Padre Pio to come by, in the hallway that led to his cell. They were all on their knees. Some of them asked for help, some wanted to kiss his hand, and others had an envelope with a donation for the hospital. He put his hand on everyone's head. I did not want to kneel down, but I also did not want to be the only one standing, so I imitated everybody else. When Padre Pio was in front of me, rather than caressing me, he hit me firmly with his fingers—twice! And he hurt me! I did not realize it was his way to reproach me for my lack of faith. I did not know he was already reading inside of me.

"One night, I was driving to Foggia, and there was a bad storm. The rain did not let me see the road, and there was thunder and lightning everywhere. I was scared, but I do not know why I thought, 'I am treating Padre Pio. He will definitely protect me.' The next morning, I had an appointment with him for the usual therapy. When I walked in, he pointed his finger at me and said, 'What were you doing yesterday in the middle of that storm?' I was speechless. How did he know where I was the day before? Without meaning to, I answered, 'Thank you, Father.' I began to understand he was protecting me.

"I am aware that it can't be proven and that it's not objective, but I really perceived his protection, his hug, in everything I did. I was a young doctor with no experience, and I had the task to build a department from scratch that later became the pride of the hospital. I thought I was alone, while Padre Pio was always there, especially in the operating room.

"I remember one event. I was carrying out a salivary gland surgery. Given my lack of experience, I made a mistake, and I cut a branch of the facial nerve. I was sure, and I still am today, that I had cut it, but the patient did not suffer from any consequences. It was completely unexplainable because there should have been consequences, such as paralysis of the eye. But there was nothing. On a different occasion, I was carrying out my first laryngectomy. I was very nervous. Later, I approached the patient's wife to explain to her all the potential complications, and she was smiling. She told me, 'Do not worry; I know that it all went well because I smelled Padre Pio's scent!' And it was true; the surgery was carried out perfectly.

"Even though everything was fine in San Giovanni Rotondo, I wanted to go back to Padoa. But while I was there, trying to convince Professor Arslan to let me come back, a strange thing happened. I got a telegram from San Giovanni. It said, 'Padre Pio needs you. Please come back.' I drove all night, and the next morning, I was at *Casa Sollievo*. I was worried, and I asked the healthcare director, 'What happened?' 'Nothing,' he replied. 'What about the telegram?' 'Which telegram?' he asked. Nobody in the hospital or in the monastery knew about the telegram: it was never sent. Padre Pio clearly wanted me to stay close to him."

14

Kisses on the Cheeks

The name of Professor Bruno Pavone is remembered and esteemed in San Giovanni Rotondo. Before his death in 2007, he had been the head physician of the maternity ward at *Casa Sollievo della Sofferenza* for forty years. He was devoted to Padre Pio, and he often spent time with him. He was also one of the witnesses called by the ecclesiastical court in Manfredonia for the beatification trial.

In order to describe the friendship between Professor Pavone and the friar, I had a long chat with his niece, Brunella Pia Pavone, who lives in Campobasso.

Brunella explained to me, "Padre Pio wanted my uncle to work in his hospital. He recommended that he study gynecology because he would later need him. When my uncle was only thirty-three years old, in 1966, Padre Pio entrusted the obstetrics ward to him. My uncle worked there until his retirement. Padre Pio was like a family member for us. My Uncle Bruno always talked about him and his good actions; I grew up listening to his stories. When I was child, I was taken to San Giovanni Rotondo, but I only have fuzzy memories of Padre Pio at the altar on that day.

"My uncle met Padre Pio in 1953 when my uncle was still a college student in Rome. He had heard about him, and he had read several articles in the newspapers about the friar from San Giovanni Rotondo. One day, he decided to meet him in person, and he was very impressed. He became a spiritual son, and he used to visit him once or twice, in order to 'oxygenate himself spiritually,' as my uncle said. Every time he had to make an important decision, he visited Padre Pio. When Padre Pio asked him to be one of the head physicians at *Casa Sollievo*, at first my uncle refused because he thought it was too much. Padre Pio acted as if nothing had happened. But after some time, he insisted, and he convinced my uncle that it was God's will. My uncle also told me that when he left his house and his mother to move to San Giovanni Rotondo, he made a big sacrifice. For this reason, Padre Pio treated him like a son. He wanted my uncle to kiss him on the cheek each time they greeted each other, in order to show him his affection for him.

"Given his proximity to Padre Pio, my uncle realized that his main concern was to perfect the penitents' souls. In order to do so, he was usually sweet, but when it was necessary, he could also be resolute and tough. My uncle said that Padre Pio was a psychologist. He knew how to evaluate the person in front of him so that he could use the best strategy. From his medical point of view, my uncle was always impressed by Padre Pio's health condition. He said it was impossible to evaluate Padre Pio's body because there was something about him that could not be understood. Sometimes he looked incredibly exhausted, while other times he recovered inexplicably.

"The day before Padre Pio's death, Uncle Bruno went to say goodbye to him because he was leaving to go on a pilgrimage to Lourdes. Padre Pio asked him, 'Are you leaving for Rome?' My uncle replied, 'No, Father, I am going to Lourdes. You know that.'

But he stopped in Rome, as Padre Pio had said. He found out about his death in Rome, and he immediately went back."

Even though Brunella Pavone did not know Padre Pio very well, her relationship with him was always very special. She told me about it in detail, and her story is really incredible.

"When I was forty years old, I looked like a woman who had succeeded. I owned a studio of interior design, which was very successful. I also worked for the Ministry of Culture. I was married, and I had two children and everything I could have wished for. But I was not happy. I was living a sort of spiritual crisis: I kept wondering what I was doing for other people. I was feeling better only when I prayed. I pretended nothing was wrong for a while, but then I could no longer stand it. I discussed it with my husband. He said, 'This is your life, and you should do what you prefer.' Three days later, I shut down my studio. I kept working at the Ministry of Culture, but I had much more free time for others.

"It was 1987. I started taking care of the children of the parish. I often told them about Padre Pio, and I even decided to go on a pilgrimage with them to San Giovanni. A little girl could not join us because she was sick. She asked me if I could bring her two small medals of Padre Pio, one for her and one for her best friend. I promised her I would, but then I was so busy that I forgot. When I came back home, I looked everywhere. I checked every drawer to see if there were any medals. I only had the one I was wearing, in my necklace, which showed an old Padre Pio. I was holding it in my hands, and it suddenly fell down. In that moment, I smelled an intense scent of roses. I looked down on the floor, where there were two small medals. I burst into tears. I immediately called Fr. Tarcisio, my confessor, who had met Padre Pio. He laughed and said, 'Padre Pio called you! Now it is your business!'

"From then on, he has never left me. I often smelled his fragrance, and when I prayed, I could hear his voice encouraging me. I began attending Mass frequently at the monastery of San Giovanni. My spiritual mentors were Fr. Gerardo de Flumeri, Fr. Marciano Morra, and Fr. Innocenzo, who had been Padre Pio's friends and brothers. I was in charge of organizing the vigils with hundreds of participants. Then I realized we needed someone who could sing and liven up the vigils. One day, in a small room of the monastery, I found an old box containing a book of songs. Padre Pio's scent immediately enveloped me, and I heard a clear voice, saying, 'You will become famous, and you will travel around the world!' I was petrified. I could not understand what Padre Pio actually wanted from me. One night, however, while I was in front of the tabernacle, rather than praying, I started singing. I had never done it before! The music and the lyrics were spontaneous. Fr. Gerardo suggested that I record the songs. People got emotional when they listened to them. I began giving concerts in Italy and abroad: in Arizona, Australia, Argentina, Canada, just like Padre Pio had told me. In Canada, I took part in a miraculous recovery.

"I still get goose bumps when I talk about it. The friars of San Giovanni gave me a few relics of Padre Pio, such as one of the gloves he used to cover the stigmata. One night, a dear friend of mine had a dream about Padre Pio. He told her, 'Tell Brunella that my glove will heal a blind child.' She told me about her dream, but I did not know what to do because I did not know any blind children. Time went by, and in 2001, I was in Toronto, Canada, to give a concert for a thousand people. I was staying at a lady's house, a spiritual daughter of Padre Pio. Suddenly there was an intense fragrance of pansies. I did not say anything at first, but then I realized that also the lady could smell it. She said, 'What a great scent. Do you smell it too?' The dream came back to my mind. I asked the lady if she knew any blind children. 'Marcus!

My cousin's grandchild. He is a few months old, and he is blind!' Before going on stage, I put the glove in the baby's romper. When the concert was over, Marcus' parents approached me, crying. They said, 'We were changing his diaper. Marcus looked at us and smiled. He can see!' Twelve years later, I went back to Canada, and I met Marcus again. He was doing great; he was a nice and healthy boy!"

15

Goat Milk

Matteo Urbano was born seventy-three years ago in the historic center of San Giovanni Rotondo. He has always been a hotel manager in the village. He met Padre Pio in 1964, and he has always had a vivid memory of him.

"My uncle was Fr. Onorato Marcucci, one of Padre Pio's brothers and friends," he said. "He was his personal assistant. He was always with him; he helped him to walk and during Mass. My uncle was the one that took me to Padre Pio for the first time, and I will never forget that moment."

Fr. Onorato Marcucci died in 1989. He appears in many pictures of Padre Pio, in the monastery or at the altar. He also appears in the famous video that shows Padre Pio's last Mass. Matteo Urbano explained to me: "My brother-in-law was his sister's son, so I am one of his distant nephews. Fr. Onorato lived for several years together with Padre Pio. His superiors asked him indeed to help Padre Pio with his daily activities. Walking was difficult for him because of the sores under his feet. My uncle supported him. When Padre Pio later had to use the wheelchair, my uncle pushed it through the hallways of the monastery. My uncle was always the one that took care of him when he was sick. He disinfected and treated his stigmata. They were friends, and they often joked, making fun of each other."

Thanks to what his uncle had told him, Matteo Urbano was able to share with me details and episodes about Padre Pio. They are priceless because they come from people that lived close to him.

"My uncle often talked to me about Padre Pio. For example, he said they liked to tell jokes. Padre Pio used to call him '*bi-secolo*' ("bi-century") because he told him he had to live for a long time in order to take care of the prayer groups. Sometimes, when Padre Pio fell asleep, my uncle tried to prank him. Once, he tried to take his rosary away from him, but Padre Pio suddenly woke up and said, 'This one stays here with me!'

"He told me that once he went with his Vespa to Monte Sant'Angelo, which is 30 kilometers (19 miles) away from the village. The scooter did not have much gas, only enough for a one-way trip. He was not going to be back to the monastery in time for Mass. But my uncle had promised Padre Pio he would be there, so he started his journey back even without gas. I do not know if he trusted in Providence, but I believe that all of Padre Pio's friends were aware that they were always protected. My uncle tried to start the Vespa, and the engine started. Therefore, he began his journey. It should have taken him 90 minutes to get to San Giovanni Rotondo from Monte Sant'Angelo, but my uncle arrived at the monastery in just 10 minutes; he was perfectly on time. He could not believe it: it was like he had driven 190 kilometers per hour. He arrived on time and in spite of the fact that the gas was not enough to cover that distance!

"Those were the beautiful things that happened when you were close to Padre Pio. When he saw my uncle walking into the monastery, he laughed and asked him, 'Onorato, has a wasp stung you?' He knew everything. On a different occasion, Onorato was leaving to visit his sister. Padre Pio gave him his scarf and wanted him to wear it. My uncle said, 'Pio, it is not that cold!' 'Wear it!' he replied. When my uncle was only 100 meters (330 feet) away from the monastery, it started snowing. It was like a blizzard in the North Pole.

"My uncle also told me that St. Joseph was Padre Pio's most beloved saint. In the monastery there was a painting that portrayed him. It was in a hallway that Padre Pio walked through to go to church. One night, Fr. Onorato was with him, and he saw him stopping in front of the painting, staring at it. My uncle was calling him, but he was completely detached. Then, with tears in his eyes, he said, 'How beautiful was St. Joseph!' He had just had a vision.

"I visited him for the first time in 1964. I was sixteen years old. My uncle wanted me to go visit him, but I could not make up my mind. The truth is that Padre Pio scared me. I heard people saying he was surly and that sometimes he sent the penitents away, shouting at them. I was intimidated, but Fr. Onorato managed to persuade me. I remember it was four in the afternoon. I was in the sacristy, and I went upstairs, to his cell, and he was suddenly in front of me. He was sitting on a wicker chair on the porch. He seriously looked at me and said, 'Come here! Why are you afraid of me?' His voice was harsh, and I thought he was going to scold me. I stared at him for a while, and then I ran away! While I was running away, I heard him shouting at me, amused, 'Come back tomorrow! I will be waiting for you!'

"'No way!' I told myself. I was never going back there. But something happened inside of me. I kept thinking about it. If I really did not care, why did I keep thinking about my appointment with Padre Pio? I was confused and curious; I can't explain it. The following day, I went back to the monastery. He was still on the porch, on the chair next to the radiator. He tenderly said,

'You came, luckily! Come next to me! So tell me, what job would you like to do when you grow up?' 'I want to be an engineer!' I replied. And he told me, 'Do not quit the job you have now.' At that time, I had started working as a bartender in a hotel, and I liked it. Well, later I ended up being a hotel manager, and I managed different hotels during my career. Padre Pio already knew it.

"I started spending time with him, and I also witnessed some events. For example, Padre Pio really liked goat milk. Sometimes I went to a shepherd who owned a plot of land near the monastery. I asked him for some milk, and I took it to Padre Pio. One day, together with my uncle, Fr. Onorato, I went upstairs to his cell with the milk. Padre Pio was looking outside the window. He told me, 'Son, one day there will be a big church on that land!' That land was indeed the area where Saint Pio's big church stands today, designed by Renzo Piano.

"I also want to share an additional event. One day, at the beginning of 1966, I asked him, 'Dear Father, many people can smell your fragrance; why can't I?' He looked at me, thoughtful, 'You start asking important things! You need to earn the scent. You have to pray. You will smell it in thirty years!' Time went by, and it was 1996. I was helping an old person that I did not know, who had to be treated at *Casa Sollievo della Sofferenza*. He was alone, and he had no family, so I acted like he was a relative of mine. I helped him, thanks to my acquaintances in the hospital, and he had the opportunity to be treated quickly. I had his situation on my heart. I even took him to the hospital and waited for him while he was having his tests done. In that moment, while I was sitting in the waiting room, I smelled a great fragrance: intense, sudden, a flowery downpour. I got emotional, and I started crying. 'You finally remembered me, Padre Pio!' I said in tears. Thirty years had gone by since his promise. How much in advance could he foresee the future?

"I never forgot that scent. Sometimes, when I pray, I still ask him, 'Dear Father, what about your scent? Only once?' I know that, sooner or later, he will answer me."

16

Always in Dialect

For a long time, I wished to meet one of Padre Pio's close relatives, somebody who belongs to his family, not one of his spiritual children or a convert. I wanted to meet one of his blood relatives because I wanted to find out his personal side, the one reserved for his family. Ten years ago, I was very happy when I had the chance to spend an afternoon with Pia Forgione, Padre Pio's niece, the daughter of his brother Michele. Mrs. Pia died in 2014. She was born in 1924, and after the war, she married Mario Pennelli, a teacher from San Giovanni Rotondo.

She was a kind woman but also discreet. Perhaps she was slightly annoyed by the countless questions everybody asked her about her famous uncle. I believe that being the niece of a saint loved worldwide involves both happiness and bothers.

Mrs. Pia was very nice to me, even though she was not particularly talkative. She explained herself: "My uncle did not talk much about himself. He would not be happy if I talked too much about him." We were in the old area of Pietrelcina, Rione Castello, where Padre Pio was born. It is a really mystical place, not austere as a cathedral. Houses are still made of stones, close to each other like puppies when they sleep. The view in the valley is the same that Padre Pio enjoyed when he was still the little Francesco.

"He was like a very caring dad," Pia Forgione told me. "He was a simple person, close to his hometown, his family, and his friends. He was very close to his brother, Michele, my father, so I have always been his favorite niece. I was somehow the connection between him and Pietrelcina. He had left the village when he was thirty years old, and he never forgot it. My uncle was very happy when somebody from Pietrelcina visited him. He kept asking if there was news about places, streets, people, and friends. He wanted to know which babies were born, who had received their First Communion, who had gotten married, and who had died. He remembered everything, even people's nicknames. During all his life, my uncle always spoke his native dialect, which showed how close he was to his hometown. He spoke his dialect also when he was with celebrities, politicians, or famous scientists.

"My uncle foresaw my birth. My father had his first son in 1909. He was named Francesco, after Padre Pio. Everybody called him Franceschino, and he was an adorable child. Padre Pio really loved him and mentioned him in many of his letters. Unfortunately, the child died when he was only eleven years old, and my parents were in despair. My father often visited Padre Pio in San Giovanni Rotondo. He told him about his heartache because he was not having other children. Padre Pio told him not to worry: he and his wife were going to become parents soon. A few months later, my mother found out she was pregnant. But that baby also died, on November 5, 1921, the day he was born. Mom and Dad were inconsolable. However, Padre Pio kept telling them to have faith because a baby was on the way. This is what Maria Pompilio, a spiritual daughter of Padre Pio, told me. He had told her, 'Get ready; you are going to be a godmother soon.' Then I was born, and Maria was my godmother. I was called Pia after my uncle.

"As I said, he was very close to his hometown. On August 21, 1962, there was an earthquake in Pietrelcina and in other villages of the Irpinia area. Several houses were damaged, especially here in Rione Castello, the oldest part of the town. They were centuries-old houses, built on rocks, without a base. They were made of stones and mortar. For this reason, the earthquake damaged them. But the municipality had no funds to fix them, so they were blocked off, and orders were given to demolish them. Padre Pio was still alive, he was well-known, but he was not a recognized saint yet. Nobody could think that later, his birth house would become a destination for many pilgrims. Those houses in Pietrelcina were about to disappear, but my uncle intervened. He called me and said, 'Pia, go to Pietrelcina and fix everything. Jesus was there; everything took place there!' These words, which I remember perfectly, are very important. They refer to all the exceptional events that took place there. In that house, indeed, my uncle had several heavenly visions when he was a child and even later. In 1909, when he got sick, he had been a monk for six years. For the following seven years, until 1916, he lived in his family house in Rione Castello. During those years, many mystical episodes occurred. He spent entire nights praying, and Jesus, Virgin Mary, and the saints constantly visited him. He also got the stigmata. This is why he told me, 'Everything took place there.'

"I went to the village, as he had asked me, and I did everything I could. I went to the region and asked for the annulment of the demolition. We were granted it, as long as we renovated the old buildings. The renovations began, and Padre Pio was really happy. He kept asking me about it. The houses belonged to us until his death. Later, we gave them up to the Capuchin monks so that they could handle them better.

"This was a foresight, too. My uncle had indeed foreseen that Pietrelcina would turn into a religious place for millions of pilgrims. For this reason, not just for personal ones, he wished to renovate the Forgione family's houses. Once, he told me, 'I valued San Giovanni while I was alive. I will value Pietrelcina when I will be dead.' In a letter to one of his followers from Pietrelcina, he wrote, 'Our village, which we love so deeply, will be blessed from the sky.'"

17

"I Used to Pull His Beard."

I was lucky to meet another relative of Padre Pio. He also described him intimately and affectionately. His first sentence was: "When I was a child, I used to pull his beard ..."

Vincenzo Masone is a fifty-eight-year-old businessman from Pietrelcina. He works in the private mail service and in catering. However, he is very well-known in the village because he is one of the creators of the famous live nativity scene. For the last thirty years, it has been set up in the old part of Pietrelcina, where Padre Pio was born. Every year, many enthusiastic tourists go admire it. His grandfather, whose name was also Vincenzo, married one of Padre Pio's sisters, Felicita. "I am the grandson of Padre Pio's brother-in-law" he says. "I grew up in Tuscany, but every summer I visited him with my family. We tenderly called him *Uncle Pio*."

"My grandfather married Felicita Forgione, Padre Pio's sister, in 1910. Padre Pio had four sisters. Amalia was born in 1885, but she died when she was still little, a few months before the birth of Francesco (Padre Pio), so he never met her. Felicita was two years younger than him, born in 1889. They were almost equal in age, and this is why Padre Pio felt closest to Felicita. The other two sisters were Pellegrina, born in 1892, and Grazia, the youngest, who was six years younger than Padre Pio. Grazia became a nun. She joined the *Ordine del Santissimo Salvatore di Santa Brigida* in Rome.

"As I said, Felicita was the sister with whom Padre Pio most got along with. They were always together as children. When he remembered his childhood, Padre Pio often talked about her and how he teased her. For example, when she was busy washing her hair, he approached her from behind, he grabbed her head, and he pushed it in the basin full of water. She told him, 'Francì! Would you stop?' But she never got mad. One day, Padre Pio said to Felicita's son, 'Your mother was the best, the kindest, and the most beautiful of the family. She was a saint. I never saw your mother upset; she was always smiling.'

"Unfortunately, his beloved sister had a difficult life. My grandfather and Felicita had three children. Giuseppina, the oldest, died of tuberculosis when she was eighteen months old. Pellegrino, the second son, died of Spanish flu when he was only four years old. That same year, in 1918, Felicita also got sick. Nothing could be done for her; she died when she was just twenty-nine years old. Grandpa Vincenzo was widowed with his two-year-old son, Ettore, who was epileptic. Perhaps Padre Pio described his sister as a saint also because of all these misfortunes.

"Her death pierced him. At that time, he was already in San Giovanni Rotondo. On October 7, 1918, he wrote a letter to his spiritual daughter Margherita Tresca: 'I have found out I have lost a sister and a nephew. ... I will let you imagine the pain I feel in my heart.' He was really heartbroken.

"Grandpa Vincenzo had become a member of Padre Pio's family. Padre Pio later loved him and was happy when he got married again a few years later. My grandfather married Giuseppa Forgione, who is my grandmother. She had the same last name as Padre Pio because she was a distant relative of his. They had three children, one of which was my father, Pellegrino. Grandpa Vincenzo died when he was fifty-five years old, in 1941. My grandmother was alone with three children and Ettore, my grandfather's son from his first marriage. It was a tragic situation: she was a woman, alone with three little children and a young boy who was sick. But Padre Pio made a deal with Grandma Giuseppa. He would take care of the education of the three children while she cared for Ettore, who was epileptic and needed special care. My father and his other siblings were sent, then, to a boarding school near Florence, in Calenzano. They studied and learned a trade. One became a typographer, one became a carpenter, and another one chose to be a tailor.

"During World War II, Calenzano was a target for bombings because there was a railway yard. However, for some 'strange' reason, no bombs ever went off near the school where Padre Pio's nephews studied. That place enjoyed his special protection. Grandma Giuseppa then moved to San Giovanni Rotondo, and my family that lived in Prato visited her every summer. That is how I met Padre Pio.

"My first clear memory of Padre Pio dates back to 1967, when I was four years old. He was 'Uncle Pio' for us. I used to sit on his lap, and I have never forgotten the kindness that enveloped me. During his last years, his beard was long and messy. I grabbed it with my little hands and asked him, 'Why don't you cut it, Uncle Pio?' He smiled, and he let me play with it; he did not tell me to stop. He hugged me, and he took a small box of candy out of the pocket of his tunic. He always gave me some of those long peppermints. Another trait of Padre Pio was the fact that he smelled good: it was a clean smell. He also slightly smelled of tobacco. Sometimes he liked to take snuff. He kept the tobacco in a little box. If you wanted to give him a nice gift, you had to bring him some tobacco from Benevento. He loved to receive typical products of his region: bread, artichokes, olive oil from Pietrelcina, and even tobacco, because in our area, it has been grown since the eighteenth century.

"Padre Pio used to tell a funny episode about his introduction to smoke. He was ten years old, and he was in the countryside. His Uncle Pellegrino told him, 'Francì, you have good feet. Here is the money; go to the village, and buy me a Tuscan cigar and a box of matches. Quickly!' Francesco did it, but on his way back, he thought, 'Let's see what smoking tastes like …' He lit the cigar in the same way he had seen his uncle doing several times. You are not supposed to inhale the smoke of a Tuscan cigar, but he immediately inhaled it deeply in his lungs, and he did not feel well. Padre Pio used to say, 'It seemed to me that the world was turning upside down …' It took him a while to feel better, and then, he slowly went back to his uncle. He told him what had happened, and his uncle burst out laughing. From then on, he never smoked again; he only took snuff every now and then."

18

Friendly Jokes

What was Padre Pio like as a child? Who did he play with? What kinds of jokes did he make? It seemed impossible to find someone who could answer these questions, but I found the right person in Pietrelcina. There I met Mrs. Maria Scocca, the granddaughter of Mercurio Scocca, Padre Pio's best childhood friend.

The name of Mercurio Scocca is often mentioned in the biographies of Padre Pio. He was his playmate, his childhood friend. He witnessed all those wonders that occurred around Francesco Forgione (Padre Pio) when he was still a child. Mrs. Maria confirmed everything: her grandfather had told her many stories.

"My grandfather Mercurio was Padre Pio's best friend, or even more. Once he grew up, Padre Pio christened Mercurio's children, and he was also their godfather. The two friends became therefore '*compari*' (old mates), a bond that in Southern Italy is still very important nowadays. He used to tell my grandfather, 'You do not have to call me Padre Pio; you should call me *compare* Pio!'"

Mrs. Scocca lives in a beautiful house outside of Pietrelcina, surrounded by the countryside. We spent an entire morning together. We had coffee, she made me try some typical home-made sweets, and she showed me a few pictures of her grandfather. Then we talked in the garden, in the shade of centuries-old trees. The lawn surrounding us was so green that it seemed to be in Ireland.

Maria explained to me: "The Scocca family was Francesco Forgione's second family. He and Mercurio were both born in 1887, and they also died in the same year, in 1968. My family lived in Piana Romana, a few kilometers away from Pietrelcina, where the Forgione family had a piece of cultivated land. Every morning, Grazio, Francesco's father, woke up at three in the morning and went to church. Then he left with his donkey for the countryside, where he worked the whole day. A few hours later, his wife, Peppa, and his son, Francesco, joined him. In the evening, the couple went back to Pietrelcina, while Francesco stayed in Scocca with his friend Mercurio and his family. They slept, ate, played, went to school, and looked after the sheep together.

"My grandfather told me he was not very happy to sleep with Francesco because he used to pray the whole night, and that kept him awake. Mercurio would tell him: 'Francè! Tomorrow we have to graze the sheep, and then we have to go to school … First you pray to Saint Lucy, then to Saint Pellegrino … I mean it; stop!'

"They were really good friends, and they also played lots of jokes on each other. For example, when people harvested wheat, they later left it in the large farmyard. It was necessary to keep an eye on it, even at night, to avoid someone stealing it. The watching was usually a task for young kids. One night, it was Francesco's shift. He dug a niche in the wheat, and he fell asleep in that sort of den. My grandpa, Mercurio, saw him, and he patiently waited for him to fall asleep. Then, he plugged him inside, sealing the exit with several armfuls of wheat. Francesco found himself buried under the wheat and got scared, but Mercurio was laughing out loud. Francesco decided to get him back, and he waited for a good opportunity. That occurred when it was Mercurio's turn to keep an eye on the wheat. He was lying on a cart, and he slowly fell asleep. Francesco untied the cart, he pushed it to the edge of a hill, and he let it go. The cart gained speed, and Mercurio was on it, screaming. He almost ended up in a trough.

"The two friends grazed sheep together. They took them to an area far from Piana Romana, to a plot of land that was used to feed animals. However, when they got there, Francesco and Mercurio used to start playing and forget about the sheep. The animals left the plot of land and went browsing in the neighboring fields that, on the contrary, were farmed. More than once, the farmers complained.

"Francesco later decided to become a monk. In 1903 he moved for his novitiate to the monastery of Morcone, 30 kilometers (19 miles) away from the village. Mercurio often asked to visit him. At that time, monasteries were supported with gifts. People used to give wine, olive oil, and some wheat from the harvest to the friars. They would also bring them parts of pork once it was butchered. For the Scocca family, it was a good opportunity to visit Francesco. My grandfather told me about a very strange episode that happened one day. He had taken some cheese to Francesco, who wanted to return the favor. Francesco picked up some chestnuts and put them in a sack. He asked my grandfather to deliver them to Mercurio's mother, who had stayed home and that he tenderly called 'Mamma Daria.' When she got the chestnuts, my great-grandmother Daria put them in the oven to toast them. She left the sack next to the oven.

"One morning, when she turned on the oven again, my great-grandmother's face and hair caught fire. She started screaming, her husband rushed to her, and he grabbed the first object he found: it was the sack that had contained Francesco's chestnuts. He used it to extinguish the flames that were enveloping his wife.

And he realized that his wife's face, skin, and hair were completely fine: there were no burns. Nobody could explain it. After some time, Mercurio went back to Morcone to bring some sweets to Francesco. While they were talking, Francesco said, 'Tell Mamma Daria I had her hair permed!' It is amazing because it proves that back then, Francesco was already capable of working miracles.

"After becoming a priest in August 1910, Francesco (who had become Padre Pio) spent a lot of time in the village because he was always sick. Mercurio made fun of him and told him, 'Francè! There is only one cure for your pain … a woman!' Padre Pio got mad and ran after him with a pitchfork.

"In 1910, Padre Pio got the stigmata, in Piana Romana, under an elm. He wished they would disappear, but he accepted to keep suffering. He did not want people's attention, but, at the same time, he did not want to give up suffering for Jesus. God fulfilled his wish, and the stigmata basically disappeared. In the biographies of Padre Pio, the stigmata of 1910 are described as invisible because they disappeared. But they did not vanish completely. Grandpa Mercurio told me that you could indeed see a red mark on Padre Pio's palm and that, especially on Fridays, he used to nervously shake his hands because they were burning. He was annoyed and told him: 'Francè, stop with those hands; it looks like you are a dancing tarantella!'

"When I was born in 1947, Padre Pio was in San Giovanni Rotondo. We often visited him. He baptized me, and in 1958, he was there for my First Communion. He had decided that it had to be on Epiphany (January 6). My father could not be there, so Michele, Padre Pio's brother, took his place. I clearly remember seeing Padre Pio without his gloves. One of his hands was holding the goblet, while with the other one, he handed out the host. I saw the light passing through his palm, from one side to the other. The stigmata actually consisted in holes that went through his hands.

"Grandpa Mercurio and Padre Pio were friends throughout their whole lives. They died the same year, just a month apart. My grandfather was very sick, and he asked to have a big portrait of his friend in his bedroom. He looked at it all the time. And he died looking at that picture."

19

Artichokes of Pietrelcina

Alberto Orlando had turned one hundred years old a few days before I met him, but he was bursting with energy. In Pietrelcina, he goes by the name of Zi' Alberto, and he is a real institution. He has always lived in Piana Romana, a few kilometers away from the village where Padre Pio's family owned a farm and a plot of land. Despite his age, Alberto works every day in the fields with his tractor. If you approach him and ask him about Padre Pio, he will be happy to share several stories with you. He proudly told me, "I was one of Padre Pio's friends. I often visited him in San Giovanni Rotondo. He loved me because I came from Piana Romana, a place he really liked and that he called *Chià Romana*. He always asked me to bring him olive oil and artichokes from here.

"People from Piana Romana got a special treatment when they visited him in San Giovanni. This village was important to Padre Pio because it was the place of his first mystical experiences and of his visions of Jesus, the Virgin Mary, and the saints. He kept repeating, 'Jesus was there! It all happened there!' Whoever came from Piana Romana had a special place in his heart. When people brought him olive oil, bread, and artichokes from his native land, Padre Pio was always very happy but not because he would have eaten them (he actually never ate much). The reason for his happiness was that those flavors reminded him of his home and childhood. The friars of the monastery in San Giovanni Rotondo tried to make him eat more. They told him the food was made with ingredients coming from Pietrelcina, but they did not fool him. He knew everything. However, he was touched by their concern, so he tasted some more food.

"People that came from his village, whether to talk to Padre Pio, or to confess to him, took advantage of a sort of fast track. There were many penitents, it was necessary to book in advance, and the line was always endless. But if you told the friars that you were from Pietrelcina or, even better, Piana Romana, you immediately had priority. They knew that was what Padre Pio wanted. We, fellow countrymen, visited him for every kind of reason. Some asked him if they should get married, while others asked him if they should plant a tree or butcher a cow or not. Students, for example, asked for his help to pass the exams, while newlyweds wanted to get his blessing to have children. Padre Pio replied to everyone, he gave suggestions, or he gave predictions that later always turned out to be accurate. Eventually, he asked specific questions about his village. He wanted to know who was born, who had received First Communion, who got married, and who had died. On those occasions he always spoke in dialect, the one he used while he grew up: it sounded like music to him.

"In 1941, I was called to join the army. The ones that belonged to my generation were sent to Russia or Africa, and I was worried. I was scared, so I visited Padre Pio in San Giovanni. I talked to him about it. He said, 'Do not worry! You are not going to leave.' I trusted him, and I went to Naples, where I found out that I was going to be sent to Avellino, just 50 kilometers (31 miles) away from home! Padre Pio was like that: he was always close to you, even if he was far.

"He asked to build a chapel in Piana Romana, in the place where he got the 'invisible' stigmata in 1910. And we fulfilled his wish. It was a meeting place, especially for those from Piana Romana. We often gathered there for the Rosary. One evening, there were twenty of us. We were praying when suddenly there was a very violent storm. The lightning lit up the countryside as if it were daytime, and the thunder shook the ground. The wind was freezing, and it was pouring. We were scared, so we moved under a tree, shivering. Suddenly, we smelled an intense scent, like a thousand roses. I immediately realized that Padre Pio was there with us. We calmed down, and we kept saying the Rosary. When it stopped raining, we looked at each other, and we were astounded: nobody got wet! It was incredible! Some time later, I visited Padre Pio in San Giovanni. As soon as he saw me, he asked me, laughing, 'Is it cold when you say the Rosary in Chià Romana?' I told him then that we smelled the fragrance. He kept laughing. 'You also smelled Padre Pio's famous fragrance!'

"The well in Piana Romana, in front of the chapel, was also commissioned by Padre Pio. In that place, Francesco used to graze sheep, and before his studies, he helped his father in the fields. Grazio, his dad, used to curse when he got mad, and Francesco obviously did not like it. One day, Grazio wanted to find water to irrigate the vegetable garden. He dug in different spots, but he could not find it. He was tired and frustrated, and he started cursing. In order to stop him, Francesco told him, 'Dig over there, in that spot!' Grazio followed his directions, and the water immediately gushed."

20

A Holy Cousin

Professor Manfredi Saginario's and Padre Pio's grandmothers were sisters. "His parents' house bordered ours," he said. "He advised me to become a doctor. I wanted to be a monk and leave on missions."

Professor Saginario was born in 1927 in Pietrelcina, but he has been living in Parma since 1935. He is also famous abroad because he is brilliant when it comes to neurological and mental diseases. He is a neurologist, psychiatrist, neuropsychiatrist, and psychotherapist, and he is a legend in Parma. "Without Padre Pio, perhaps my fate would have been different." This is one of the first things he told me when I visited him.

"The first time I met Padre Pio, I was eighteen years old. I had never met him before because when I was born, he had already been living in San Giovanni Rotondo for ten years. My teacher was Angelo Caccavo, the same teacher that Padre Pio had had. My parents and I then moved to Parma after my first year of primary school. I grew up always hearing about Padre Pio. Every summer, we went back to Pietrelcina, and my grandparents told me amazing facts about our relative, who was so well-known. They told me, 'Behave, or otherwise Padre Pio will be sad!'

"Our first meeting was very exciting. But I have to admit that we also had disagreements. When I was young, I wanted to become a missionary. I felt the urgency to go to Third World countries to help and comfort the people living there. But at the same time, I also had many doubts. My parents told me to visit Padre Pio and to ask him for advice. Actually, they forced me to visit him because I did not want to. Two of my aunts came with me. They made me sleep in their room because they feared I would run away during the night and go back home. I have always had a rebellious and nonconformist personality. I did not like the fact that I had been forced to visit Padre Pio. I told myself, 'How can he tell me what I have to do with my life?' I was young, and I did not trust him that much. But later I changed my mind.

"As soon as he saw me, he said, 'There he is! You finally came!' He talked as if we had had an appointment that I had often postponed. I realized he knew everything about me. He had been informed about what I did in Parma, how my grades were at school, and if I was behaving like a good Catholic. My aunts from Pietrelcina often visited him, and they had informed him about every single detail. He knew, for example, that I had joined the *Azione Cattolica* association, that I had founded a Catholic association in Parma, and that I regularly went to the senior center to help. He also knew that, when I was in Pietrelcina during wartime, I had founded a Catholic association also there, in which almost all the young people of the village were involved. He was happy about all that.

"Then he asked me why I was visiting him. I admitted that I was a little bit embarrassed. I was sorry to bother him, but my parents had insisted on asking him advice. Padre Pio smiled and explained to me that people visited him for different reasons. Some of them asked him if it was a good idea to get married, while others wanted to know if they had to grow wheat or buy a pig or a cow. He told me he was happy to talk to me because I was part of the family.

"I told him I wanted to become a missionary, but I also had doubts because I would liked to get married and have children. He was not perplexed. He said, 'Create your own family. Be a doctor; you will still be able to help others. You will succeed. We need missionaries, but we also need doctors to help the patients!' And that is what I have been doing my whole life.

Because of my personality, I always pointed out what I did not like, so I did the same on that occasion. As soon as he saw me, Padre Pio told me to confess. He did not suggest that people confess; he basically ordered you to do it. He would say, 'Welcome. Come to confess!' My penance was to recite seven Our Fathers, seven Hail Marys, and seven Glory Be's. I was stunned. I thought my penance was too harsh because I did not feel like I had committed many sins. The next day, I told him, 'Father, I did not follow your directions regarding the penance.' His face became severe: 'There is a devil in my family!' He let me be because he loved me.

"I started visiting him at least once a year. I also organized pilgrimages, bringing other people. Padre Pio was proud of me. He was proud of the fact that someone in his family could become a doctor (all the others were farmers). It was really important to him. He showed interest in my studies, and he told me, 'Do not miss this chance. You are the pride of the family.' Every time he wanted to know what was going on in Pietrelcina, but I lived in Parma, so I did not know. My friends in Pietrelcina had to inform me, or I had to stop by the village on my way from Parma to San Giovanni Rotondo. I was sure he would ask me for news, so I had to be ready. But I am sure he already knew everything; he was always aware of everything. He hoped I kept in touch with people from Pietrelcina. When I was not aware of something about the village, he was surprised and perplexed. Then he would ask me,

'Aren't you from Pietrelcina?' 'Yes, Father, but I live in Northern Italy.' And he would say, 'I know you live in the North, but aren't you from Pietrelcina?' Even if you lived far away, it was unimaginable for him to not be in touch with your native town.

"Before moving to Parma, we were the neighbors of Padre Pio's family. Grazio Forgione and Maria Giuseppa lived in Pietrelcina, in Vicolo Storto, a small uphill street. Our house was just a few meters away. We lived next to the church of *Santissima Annunziata*, where Padre Pio had celebrated Mass when he was younger, and where he often had mystical experiences. Our families were also neighbors in the countryside. Both my family and Grazio Forgione had a plot of land in Piana Romana, an area just outside of the village. The two properties bordered, and they shared the same farmstead, which was simply divided into two parts. And in the fields, near a barn, there was the famous elm under which Padre Pio got the stigmata in 1910.

"My grandfather Manfredi was the one who told me the most about him. They were friends, even though my grandfather was not a very religious person. He was a locksmith, and he used to curse. But he had a big heart, and he felt sorry for that friar because not everyone in the village was nice to him. Padre Pio lived in Pietrelcina from 1910 until 1915 because some of his undiagnosed diseases forced him to stay home. Every time he left the village, he would get sick, while every time he went back to Pietrelcina, he quickly recovered. People in the village said he was affected by tuberculosis, but it was not true. People were just afraid because tuberculosis was a very scary disease. For this reason, Padre Pio was somehow isolated. My grandfather told me that people would not let him come in their houses. Somebody even put a chair outside the door and talked to him through a window. But it was not my Grandpa Manfredi's case: he always let him in. Padre Pio usually spent four hours praying on his knees in the church.

"When he left the church in the winter, he was almost frozen. Nobody was at his house because his family was in the fields, so he stopped by my grandfather's house. He let Padre Pio sit next to the brazier to warm. He also offered him some soup, but Padre Pio always refused because, according to the Franciscan rule, he could not accept food from a secular person. When he heard my grandfather cursing, he scolded him: 'Control your mouth!' And my grandfather, who could not hold his tongue, would reply, 'Father, I do not curse. I simply review the saints' names!'"

21

Touching Tenderness

Primo Capponcelli was a distinguished gentleman from Bologna who had the good fortune of being one of Padre Pio's friends. He lived in San Matteo della Decima, near San Giovanni in Persiceto and Bologna. He had been very close to Padre Pio for eight years. He visited him hundreds of times, taking many people to him. Their tender friendship lasted until Padre Pio's death in 1968. Primo Capponcelli's testimony is amazing because it includes both the story of a miraculous recovery and the incredible daily episodes that took place around the friar with the stigmata.

Capponcelli told me, "I met Padre Pio in 1959. One of my relatives had sent me a postcard with the friar's picture on it. I had honestly never heard about him. I put it in the drawer of the desk without thinking, and every time I opened it, Padre Pio was there. One day, a friend from Modena told me he was planning a trip to San Giovanni Rotondo to visit Padre Pio, and he asked me if I wanted to join them. 'I will gladly come,' I replied. 'I see his picture every day when I open my drawer. I will finally be able to meet him.'

"Once I got there, I did what everybody else was doing. I scheduled my confession with Padre Pio for two days later. While I was waiting, I heard incredible stories about him, so I was very curious. When I walked in, Padre Pio glared at me, and his gaze was scary. He said, 'Go away.' I did not expect such a treatment, and I did not know what to say, so I silently left. Then I found out that Padre Pio often behaved like that. If you wanted to confess only so that you could see him, he knew it. He could read your heart, and he got angry if you did not actually repent of your sins. I realized that was what I had done. I was ashamed. I went back home, and a month later, I had another opportunity to go to San Giovanni. I attended Mass at five in the morning, and then I went to the sacristy where Padre Pio used to welcome people. That time, I was intimidated rather than curious. I was afraid because he could have sent me away again. But he came straight to me, and said, 'What are you doing there? Come, come with me.' He took me to the confessional, and his tenderness was moving. My father had died when I was a child, and he filled that void. From then on, I often visited him. I even bought a van to take other people to him, people that were hoping to change their lives.

"In 1962, I had a bad heart attack. At that time, medicine was almost powerless when it came to this kind of emergency. The doctors were worried because my condition was severe. A friend of mine, a spiritual child of Padre Pio like me, went to San Giovanni Rotondo to ask him to pray for my health. Padre Pio was quiet for a few seconds, and then he replied, 'I will pray. Tell him not to worry; he will recover.' And it was true. Eight days later, I had other tests done, and there was no evidence of my heart attack. The doctors were surprised. They said, 'Perhaps we were wrong,' and they sent me home.

"There were other people in the hospital with me with severe heart conditions. Since I had recovered and I kept talking about

Padre Pio, they asked to be helped, too. I called Padre Pio in San Giovanni Rotondo and told him about these people. In the next week, three other patients inexplicably recovered. I can tell that Padre Pio always helped those who believed in him and whose heart was sincere.

"A friend of mine had an epileptic child. A countless number of doctors had examined him, but they all said he had no chance to recover. I took them to Padre Pio. He asked, 'Has he taken the medicine?' My friend replied, 'No, he can't swallow them.' Padre Pio touched the child and said, 'Now he will be able to take them. And he will recover soon.' Fifteen days later there was nothing wrong with the child. The doctors of the hospital of Modena, where he was treated, were shocked. That child later became a priest and never had any kind of issue.

"Once, I took a man with me who did not believe in Padre Pio's stigmata. He was Catholic, but he thought that Padre Pio was surrounded by fanaticism. He kept saying, 'The stigmata are a lie. I would like to see them in person; then I would believe.' When they met, Padre Pio stared at him intensely. He took off his gloves, showing him the stigmata, and said, 'There are still several St. Thomases in the world!'

"I had taken over a factory that was going bankrupt. However, at the time of the drafting of the contract, I had been deceived. The law about bankruptcy had not been abided by, so I ended up in court. It was a serious matter, and I risked going to jail. My lawyers were worried. I visited Padre Pio, and I told him everything. 'Father, if I go to jail, please, take care of my children …' He smiled. 'Do not worry; you won't go to jail.' Some time later I went to court for the trial, but the situation was totally different. I had turned into a simple witness. I do not know how he did it, but Padre Pio had solved everything."

22

"Go in Peace! I Already Know Everything!"

Angela Miscio is ninety-six years old. She is an elegant lady who belongs to an important family from San Marco in Lamis, where she lives, close to San Giovanni Rotondo. She has six daughters, sixteen grandchildren, and thirteen great-grandchildren.

"My brother Gabriele was a former officer in the Navy, and he was a teacher at the *Istituto Tecnico Nautico di Foggia*," she said. "He and I had had a bad fight about our family and the inheritance. I am sorry to admit it, but the situation degenerated, and eventually we were no longer in touch. We no longer talked to each other. I knew he had moved to Foggia, but we did not have a relationship; we were two strangers.

"One day I confessed to Padre Pio. I think it was 1966 or 1967. He asked me precisely, 'Are you getting along with everyone in your family?' His question surprised me, but I told him the truth: 'Yes, Father. I get along with everyone, except for my brother Gabriele.' He said, 'I can't give you absolution then. I will when you will make peace with him.'

"When I left the church, I was intimidated. You could not joke around with Padre Pio. He looked brusque, but if you had known him well, you would have realized he was not. However, when it came to certain topics, he did not compromise, and you could not do what you wanted. When he scolded you, you could pretend nothing happened, but you actually kept thinking about it day and night, as if there were a nail in your soul. I had no choice: if I wanted to get absolution, I had to reconcile with Gabriele.

"It was not easy. We were both very proud, which was why we ended up fighting. Besides, he had received a military education, so he was even more rigid. He was never going to make the first move. We were also distant: even though Foggia is only 40 kilometers (25 miles) away from here, it was not easy to get there at that time. Moreover, I had six daughters, my days were really busy, and it was hard to find the time to plan a trip to the city. But even if I had had the time, I did not know where Gabriele lived. I knew nothing: his street, his address, or his phone number.

"I am sure Padre Pio intervened. One day, one of my daughters, who studied at the University of Bari, asked me to take her to class because she did not feel well. I went with her, but it was something unusual because it had never occurred before. We went home soon after lunch. The train stopped in Foggia, and we started walking to catch the bus for San Giovanni. In a street not far from the station, we bumped into my brother! It was surprising; I could not believe it. He was very kind, he greeted us, and he invited us for some tea and pastries. We talked a lot, and we finally made peace. I found out that he was usually at home at that time and that he had never walked along that street before. He did not know why that day he had decided to turn on that street.

"The first thing I did the next morning was go to the monastery to confess to Padre Pio. I wanted to tell him what had happened and get absolution. I was waiting in line. When it was my turn, I did not even have time to bend on my knees. Padre Pio told me: 'Go in peace! I already know everything.' He gave me absolution, and I was relieved when I left.

"How could he know about it? Why did my brother leave the house at that time if it was not his habit? Especially on the day I was in Foggia. I often asked myself these questions, but I can't answer. Padre Pio's holiness also consisted of these little things, helping the penitents step-by-step, using his mysterious charisma.

"I am not sure what my brother thought on that day, but something must have happened in his heart, and he changed. He had always disapproved of the Church, and he had never had a good relationship with Christians. However, after his funeral, we found out about all the charity work he had done throughout the years. He had moved to Milan, and he had supported the *Istituto Don Orione*. Not even his children knew about it. My brother was a reserved person, and without telling anyone, he wanted to show with facts that something in his life had changed. Perhaps Padre Pio was the author of his improvement."

23

Head Bowed, Rosary in Hand

Fr. Riccardo Fabiano is eighty years old, and he is the keeper of Padre Pio's relics. He is a theologian, dean of the seminary in Campobasso, and superior of the monastery in San Giovanni Rotondo. Together with the *Associazione Amici di Pio* and *Araldi di San Pio*, he takes the relics to all the European parishes that ask to see them. I met him a few years ago in San Pietro di Marubio, in the province of Verona. He had been invited by the priest, Don Michele Fiore, to show to the worshippers a glove and also a small piece of scab that belonged to Padre Pio. The latter is a very rare relic, and there are only three pieces like that. One is at the *Curia generalizia* of the Capuchin monks in Rome, one was given to Pope John Paul II, and it is in the Vatican, while the third one is the one in San Giovanni Rotondo, looked after by Fr. Riccardo.

Father Riccardo told me, smiling, "Padre Pio belonged to God and to humankind. He was a saint, a great mystic. But when he was among us, the friars, or together with the laymen who visited him, he was simple, loving, and funny. I met him on different occasions, and his frankness when he talked always impressed me, as well as his strength while he endured his sufferings."

Fr. Riccardo was kind and helpful, and he gladly agreed to tell me about his meetings with Padre Pio. He sat and, with his hands combed his white majestic beard. He explained to me, "Nowadays, only the oldest Capuchin monks have a long beard. But it was very common in the past. Padre Pio became a friar so that he could have a long beard! When he was ten years old, he met a Capuchin monk for the first time in his life. His name was Fr. Camillo. His composure, his friendliness, and even his bushy dark beard were imprinted in Padre Pio's mind. That was when he decided to become a monk, but not any monk. He wanted to become a bearded friar. When Padre Pio remembered that episode of his childhood, he used to say, 'Fr. Camillo's beard got stuck in my mind!'

"I saw Padre Pio for the first time in 1954. I was fourteen years old, and I was attending the seminary in Avellino. Together with forty other students, I was taken to Padre Pio to get his blessing. Our superiors told us to be quiet and to not bother him. We were all standing in the hallway, waiting, without making any sound. Padre Pio came down the stairs, he turned around, and he was suddenly in front of us. He was surprised, almost scared. He shouted, 'Move a little bit! You scared me! Make some noise; otherwise, what are your superiors supposed to do?' I was told Padre Pio was strict, unfriendly, and intimidating. But because of his words, I immediately found him funny. Later, I also admired his charisma. His jokes were hilarious. They were typical of him. Carlo Campanini, the famous comical actor, was one of his close followers. He told jokes and funny stories to Padre Pio. He retold them three or four times in a row so that Padre Pio could learn them by heart and share them in the future.

"In 1965, I was asked to join a group of four or five friars in order to reply to the thousands of letters received by Padre Pio. We were authorized to write in his place. I remember a letter from Piacenza. It was from a woman asking for Padre Pio's advice and for his prayers. Satan was tormenting her. In that case, I had to talk to Padre Pio before replying, so I looked for him. He asked me, 'What do you need?' I explained the content of the letter. He said, 'You can tell her the following: my suggestion is to visit the priest of her parish in order to have some exorcisms performed. I will take care of the prayers. Tell her not to worry.'

"In the late 1960s, I was about to finish my theology studies at the *Università dei Gesuiti* in Naples. I decided to write a thesis on Fr. Benedetto Nardella from San Marco in Lamis, who had been Padre Pio's spiritual director for a long time. He had been a very important figure for the young saint. I visited Padre Pio to get his approval. I was taken to his cell, and I was left alone with him. I remember he was sitting, his head was bowed, and he was holding the rosary in his hands. It looked like he was sleeping, but he was actually praying intensely. I waited for a while, and then I said, 'I would like to write about Fr. Benedetto, your spiritual supervisor.' 'That is fine,' he replied. His answer was short and abrupt. 'Do you think it is worth it?' I asked. 'Of course!' he said. I was happy, so I ended up saying, 'Well, what is most important is that it will turn out to be a good thesis for school.' Padre Pio opened his eyes, he scrutinized me, and he said, 'What is most important is that Fr. Benedetto protects us!' That was a valuable lesson for me. I was worried about my project, while Padre Pio had drawn attention to a more important aspect: the protection of the saints in heaven.

"I met him for the last time in April 1968. He died five months later. Again, on that occasion, his natural simplicity impressed me. Back then, I was the chaplain of *Fratelli delle Scuole Cris-*

tiane, a congregation established by St. John Baptist de La Salle. I visited Padre Pio along with the members of the congregation. He blessed us, and he encouraged us to pray, not just for ourselves, but also for others. Then he added, 'Always imitate St. John the Baptist, your founder ...' He suddenly fell silent because he did not remember his entire name. We were a little embarrassed, but he calmly turned to his brothers next to him. 'What is this saint's name?' They let him know so that he could end his speech.

"I, like others, smelled the famous scent of Padre Pio. One day, I was walking through the hallway, near his cell, when I smelled an intense flower fragrance. I did not understand where it was coming from, and I remember thinking it was the paint from the radiator. A few years after Padre Pio's death, one of his former brothers, who used to keep many objects that belonged to Padre Pio, asked me if I wanted to smell the scent that many people had talked about. He took me to a room, where he took some tissues out of a drawer. Padre Pio had used them to dry the stigmata of the rib cage. I got closer, and I smelled that amazing scent. It reminded me of that afternoon, when I had smelled the same fragrance in the hallway, and I thought it was paint. It was rather the smell of the blood of the stigmata! That mystery always fascinated me, as well as those episodes of bilocation. I have never witnessed them, but I have heard incredible stories. One night, for example, Padre Pio was in his cell, but he was also seen at *Casa Sollievo della Sofferenza* comforting some sick patients. The patients told the friars about it. The friars knew that Padre Pio had never left the monastery, so they asked Padre Pio for explanations. 'Father, did you go to *Casa Sollievo* last night?' He was annoyed. 'Why? Am I not allowed to go there?' 'But you do not have the key,' they replied. 'And do you really think I need the key?'

"While I was collecting material for the book on Fr. Benedetto, I found out something very interesting. In 1922, Fr. Benedetto's superiors ordered him to stop being Padre Pio's confessor. He could no longer write to him. Fr. Benedetto obeyed until his death in 1942. He never saw or heard about Padre Pio again. During the final days of his life, he was sick at the monastery of San Severo. The friars who were taking care of him asked him if he wanted to inform Padre Pio of his health condition or if he wanted to see him. Fr. Benedetto calmly replied, 'He is already here. Can't you see him?' Padre Pio was very attached to him. I am sure he visited him more than once, thanks to bilocation, so that he could be comforted before dying."

24

"Our Lady Knows What to Do."

The transportation company Centra is well-known in San Giovanni Rotondo. It has forty employees and also has a branch in Rome. It was begun by Donato Centra in the 1960s. It was the first company that took pilgrims on a daily basis from the center of the village to the monastery where Padre Pio lived. Donato had known Padre Pio since he was a child. He had witnessed several exceptional events, such as an unexplainable recovery that occurred thanks to the friar. In order to investigate, I spoke with Donato's son, Antonio Centra, who now runs the family company.

"My father often had the chance to meet Padre Pio. Dad died in 2018, when he was eighty-eight years old. In his lifetime, he loved sharing episodes of Padre Pio's life with the pilgrims."

However, I found out that there was another reason why Donato was very well-known in the village. "His father, which is my grandfather, was Antonio Centra, and in 1922, he threatened Padre Pio with a gun. He was not a criminal, and he acted that way because of his deep love for Padre Pio. Starting from 1919, when Padre Pio's stigmata became famous, the Vatican thought about relocating him abroad. The goal was to prevent people from visiting him. They wanted to make him disappear, hide him, and make people forget about him. The citizens of San Giovanni Rotondo had heard about these plans, and they resolutely opposed them. In 1922, new orders from Rome were sent, and the people rose up. One morning, at the end of Mass, my grandfather Antonio Centra moved closer to the altar and pointed a gun at Padre Pio. He shouted, 'Rather than leaving us, I would prefer you were dead here in San Giovanni!' He did not really mean it, and he did not do anything else. This shows what kind of atmosphere there was back then and how scared people were to lose that friar, who was already believed to be a saint.

"Dad told me many stories. For example, he told me that one day, as a child, a bottle of wine was delivered at his house for Padre Pio. It came with a letter. My grandfather told my dad to take the letter to the monastery: just the letter, while he kept the wine. As soon as Padre Pio saw my father, he did not let him speak, and he said, 'You have a letter for me!' Then, referring to my grandpa who had stayed home with the wine, he added, 'Good job, *Mastro* Antonio! He sends me the letter, but he keeps the wine!' He knew everything even if he had not even opened the envelope. Padre Pio could easily read people's hearts and minds.

"My father first worked as a bricklayer. He told me that, together with his father, he left for Foggia on foot, where they stayed the whole week to work in the construction sites. It was right after World War II, and because of the bombings, there was a lot to rebuild. My dad loved cars, so he also worked in a garage. Then he worked as a truck driver for a company that carried bauxite from the mine in San Giovanni to the harbor in Manfredonia. A few years later, he decided to become self-employed. He bought a truck with a trailer, and he established the company Centra. With his truck, he transported all of the marbles for the construction of the church *Santa Maria delle Grazie*, the kind of marble Padre Pio wanted. But being a truck driver was a hard job, without a fixed schedule, and my father talked about it with Padre Pio.

"It was five in the morning, and he had just arrived at the construction site of the church. He had traveled all night from Bolzano to carry the bronze angels that support the holy water fonts. Nowadays, they still stand next to the entrance of the church. Padre Pio was celebrating Mass outdoors because there was no more space for all the pilgrims in the small church of the monastery. That is why a new church was being built. At the end of Mass, my father followed him into the sacristy. He told him that being a truck driver was exhausting and that he hoped to do something different. Padre Pio, who loved all his spiritual children, quickly replied, 'Do not worry; pray to Our Lady. She knows what to do. Things will change.' When he talked like that, it meant he would plead your case, that he would personally speak to the Virgin Mary about that matter. Soon after that, my father stopped being a truck driver. He had the opportunity to drive the village bus that carried the pilgrims to the monastery. The job was much less tiring, and later his company expanded.

"In 1962, my father witnessed an amazing recovery that took place thanks to Padre Pio. One of his nephews, his sister's son, had been recently born, but the baby was not doing well. The fontanel on his head was not healing, so a specialist had to examine him. He was admitted to *Casa Sollievo* for some tests. The pediatrician told my father that the baby would become blind. The situation was hopeless and devastating, and the baby would not stop crying. My dad was heartbroken, and he left the hospital to inform his sister about it.

"In front of the church, he met Fr. Eusebio Notte, who was Padre Pio's assistant at that time. He asked my father why he looked so sad, and my father explained everything to him. Fr. Eusebio grabbed his hand: 'Let's go immediately to Padre Pio!' They entered the monastery, went upstairs, and on the landing, they bumped into Padre Pio. Fr. Eusebio told him about the baby and the doctors' diagnosis. Padre Pio replied, 'Doctors can be wrong sometimes,' and he left. Fr. Eusebio then said, 'Donato, you can go home now' because he knew what Padre Pio meant. He meant that the baby would recover. The following day, my dad went to the hospital. The pediatrician was shocked. He was holding the most recent x-rays, and he was comparing them with those of the day before. He said, 'Everything is fine; the baby is healthy. But the x-rays show that yesterday his condition was different!' There was a nurse nearby. As soon as she heard my father's voice, she asked him, 'Donato, when have you been to Padre Pio?' My dad thought, 'How does she know I have seen him?' 'At ten,' he replied. 'That was exactly the time when the baby stopped crying,' she said. Today that baby is a professor, he is married, and he has two children. He has never had any health issues."

25

"I Think of Him When I Celebrate Mass."

I met Don Giuseppe Cenci in the village of Monteciccardo, in the hills of the Marche region. He is the priest of the church *San Sebastiano*, and he is eighty-four years old. He showed me the statue of Padre Pio that he has placed in the garden of the rectory. He told me about his meetings with the saint in the 1960s.

"This statue, with the right hand on the heart and the left hand holding the Rosary, represents Padre Pio's protection," Don Giuseppe said. "I met him for the first time in 1962. I was going through a personal crisis. I wanted to become a priest, but I was having a lot of difficulties, and my wish to dedicate myself to God was remaining unfulfilled. Padre Pio, then, in a mysterious way, made me realize the journey of my vocation would still be long and painful. But I had to resist and believe. He was going to be close to me.

"As far back as I can remember, I have always wanted to become a priest. My family, however, was poor, and I could not attend the seminary to study. We lived in Milan, and I was already working in a factory when I was fourteen years old. We needed to earn money, so I had to put aside my desire to become a priest. I had no choice, but I was not taking it well. Your vocation is not a fleeting thought or a temporary whim. It is deep in your soul, and it does not allow you to think of anything else. You know you were born to do that, and you know you will feel fulfilled only once you will be a priest. Otherwise, you suffer. I felt out of place and dissatisfied, so I decided to talk to Padre Pio.

"I had read about him, and I knew who he was because he was famous. But I had never been to San Giovanni Rotondo. At that time I thought his advice would be helpful. I remember the Mass at five in the morning and the crowded church, as well as the sacristy, with all those people, waiting to be blessed by Padre Pio. I was among them, excited. Suddenly, I smelled an intense scent of disinfectant. It was very acidic, pungent, and piercing. I looked around, and I asked the people next to me if they could smell it, too, but I realized I was the only one smelling it. I knew that Padre Pio used to reveal himself using a flower smell and that only the ones he wanted to reach could smell it. But I did not know he could also make you smell an unpleasant scent. I was told it actually happened. Some of the believers could indeed smell the odor of disinfectant or acid. It meant that a person was going to face difficult spiritual challenges. That person also had to fight with faith, but Padre Pio would be close to them. I did not know all this back then, but it was exactly what happened to me.

"That day, in the sacristy, I was in line with everybody else to kiss his hand. However, when I was in front of him, he tenderly put his hand on my head. I did not understand his gesture, but he was promising me that he was going to be there for me. In that moment, an invisible and mysterious thread brought us together.

"When I went back to Milan, I had made my decision: I was going to attend the seminary. But from that moment, everything turned out to be difficult, as if I had hit an insurmountable wall. A few months after I started attending the seminary, I had to stay for two months in the hospital because of a severe pulmonary infection. I recovered slowly. The other students were younger than me, and they had a better education, so it was hard for me to keep up with the lessons. When I eventually caught up, I experienced a retinal detachment. None of the doctors' treatments worked. I was discouraged, so I sent a letter to Padre Pio, in which I told him about my situation. I received his answer, handwritten by one of his brothers. It said, 'Padre Pio is praying.' As soon as I got the letter, I immediately began improving. The treatment, which was useless at first, became effective, and I recovered. I resumed my studies, but it was difficult because I had missed so much, and I was not in good health. The dean of the seminary was very honest with me: he told me I was not a fit for the priestly type of life. I should not have made the effort. A religious order wouldbe more appropriate for me. He sent me to the seminary of Seveso for some time, telling me he was going to think about it. But he had already decided: he was going to make me leave the seminary.

"While I was in Seveso, however, the bishop of Fossombrone, a diocese in the Marche region, visited us. When he found out that my parents were natives of Marche, he immediately liked me. And when he was informed of my situation, he told me I could attend the seminary in Fano. He said I could keep studying there and become a priest. I was so happy. My encounter with the bishop got things moving again. His visit to Seveso was providential. Was that a coincidence? Later, I found out it was not.

"The day of my ordination to the priesthood was scheduled for September 28, 1968. I spent the whole month of August in San Giovanni Rotondo. Padre Pio was old and sick, but I could feel his presence anyway. One day, I was about to leave the hotel when an intense flower fragrance enveloped me. I turned around, and there was a lady who asked me what she could do to meet

Padre Pio. A young man was with her. He was depressed, and she hoped Padre Pio could bless him. The following day, I attended the morning Mass with the young man, whose name was Pietro. Then, we waited for Padre Pio. He was in a wheelchair because he was not feeling well, and one of his brothers was pushing him. When he was in front of Pietro, he stopped, he stared at him, and he put his hand on his head. Pietro recovered immediately: he totally changed, and he left San Giovanni Rotondo smiling, like no one had seen him before.

"I saw Padre Pio again before leaving. 'Pray for me,' I said. 'On the 28th I will become a priest. And pray for my bishop.' 'Who is your bishop?' he asked. 'The bishop of Fossombrone,' I replied. I will never forget Padre Pio's face. He was both pleased and thoughtful, as if he were keeping a funny secret or remembering something nice. Looking at him there, I realized he knew everything and that the bishop's visit to Seveso was not a coincidence. It was he, Padre Pio. He smiled, he opened his arms, and he told me: 'Remember that once you become a priest, you will be at the altar forever!' I have never forgotten his words, and when I celebrate Mass, I always think about him."

26

"Did You Dare to Doubt?"

There are thousands of monuments dedicated to Padre Pio, all over Italy. There are statues of him standing or bent on his knees, smiling or praying. These statues can be found in churches, chapels, or private gardens. Some of these statues were created by a man from Bolzano. He was not a sculptor, but he unexpectedly ended up having a beautiful experience next to Padre Pio. His name was Agide Finardi. He died in 2010 when he was ninety years old. I had met him in the 1990s, and I have always kept his story, knowing that it was going to be helpful.

"I am not an artist," was the first thing he told me. "I know a lot about cars, and when I was twenty-two years old, I was already a successful car manufacturer. I owned a company called *Rondine*, and it was doing very well. When Padre Pio died, his spiritual children asked me to create some statues. They were asking me because I knew Padre Pio well enough, and I remembered his features and his facial expressions. So I attempted to create one, and it worked. I have never stopped since then.

"I met Padre Pio for the first time in 1949. I was going through a complicated situation back then. Both of my parents had cancer. I had been married for four years, but I did not have any children.

My wife and I wanted to become parents, and the fact that we did not have a baby yet saddened us. And I was worried for my parents. I felt overwhelmed. One day, I heard about Padre Pio, a friar who worked miracles. Could he help me, too? I decided to leave for Southern Italy. I arrived in San Giovanni Rotondo very early in the morning, and after Mass, I confessed to Padre Pio. I had not even opened my mouth yet, when he said, 'You went to confession yesterday morning.' It was true; I had gone in Foggia. 'I would like to confess in general,' I said. I told him about my parents, their disease, and the fact I was not having children. Padre Pio was listening, concentrating. Then he said, 'Your mom will live for another few months and your dad for a few years. You are going to have a son, Pio, and you will change your job.' It was all so precise, as if he had just read a page of his breviary. I was both relieved and doubtful. I was about to leave when Padre Pio added, 'Didn't you forget to tell me something?' I looked at him, and I immediately remembered that I had prepared a donation before the confession. I was forgetting to give it to him. I realized he always knew everything; he could read people as if they were made of glass.

"Padre Pio was right. My mother died indeed three months later. My father lived another four years. My wife got pregnant. It was a boy, and we obviously called him Pio. Padre Pio was right also about my job. For family reasons, after my mother's death, I had to leave my house and end my business. I had to start all over again, with a new job. I became a lathe turner.

"I went back multiple times to San Giovanni Rotondo, and I became one of Padre Pio's spiritual children. He wanted me to join the works of the new church that was being built in San Giovanni Rotondo. I carried out all the ironwork and bronze work. I worked in that church until his death. I witnessed amazing miracles next to him; it was like living in an imaginary world.

One evening, I left from San Giovanni Rotondo to go back to Bolzano. I was very tired, and I fell asleep while I was driving. I am not sure for how long. At some point, I was punched in my stomach, and I was breathless. I stopped the car, and 20 meters (66 feet) away, there was a railroad crossing. It was down, and the train passed through in that moment. I made a U-turn, and I drove back to San Giovanni Rotondo. I visited Padre Pio the next morning. Before I could open my mouth, he told me, 'When you are so tired, you should not drive. Do you want me to drive your car all the way home?' He was the one who punched me and saved me.

"One day, after Confession, I asked Padre Pio if he could give me some keepsakes for the people of my town. He gave me three small medals. 'Father, there are four people,' I said. He replied, 'No, one still has to convert. He can have the medal after that.' Indeed, one of these people belonged to a Protestant family.

"On another occasion, I was in Bolzano, and I was attending Mass. At that time, when the priest celebrated Mass, he did not face the faithful. When he turned around, I realized it was Padre Pio. I thought I was hallucinating, so I moved closer. It was really him. But how was it possible? When Mass was over, I ran to the sacristy, where I realized the priest was not Padre Pio. But I thought that maybe he wanted to tell me something. I drove all the way to San Giovanni Rotondo. When he saw me, Padre Pio said, 'Do I need to pick you up at home?'

"One morning, I visited him in his cell. I wanted to tell him goodbye because I was going back to Bolzano. He told me, smiling, 'The bike can be fixed. The ashtray can be made. Iron can be sold, and wine and sandwiches can be bought.' I had no idea what he was talking about. But a few days later, when I was at home, I walked in the workshop, and I noticed that the handlebars and the fenders of my bike had been cut. I remembered Padre

Pio's words, so I called one of the workers. I asked him if, by any chance, he had sold some iron and bought wine and sandwiches. He told me he had disassembled the bike to make it faster. He had made an iron ashtray, but it did not look good, so he had thrown it away. He had sold some pieces of junk, earning 2,700 lire. With that money, he had bought some sandwiches and a bottle of wine. It was exactly what Padre Pio had said.

"During my stays in San Giovanni, sometimes I helped Padre Pio when he celebrated Mass. I remember that once I had a terrible doubt. I thought that his stigmata were not real and that his hands were not actually bleeding. I started praying to stop thinking about my doubts. When it was time to pour the water and the wine, I saw a drop of blood on Padre Pio's little finger. And the drop fell in the goblet. I was scared and touched at the same time, and I spilled the water and the wine on the altar. Padre Pio glared at me. When Mass was over, he took me aside and said, 'Did you have the courage to doubt?'"

27

"Be Quiet, Agostì! Do Not Worry!"

"This handkerchief is really valuable. It belonged to my grandmother, and Padre Pio held it in his hands. For this reason, it turned into an extraordinary relic that my family devoutly keeps."

These are Celestina Orlando's words, who is forty-two years old. I met her in Pietrelcina, but she lives in Piana Romana, a few kilometers away from where Padre Pio's family worked in the countryside. Celestina showed me an old yellowed handkerchief, with several rusty stains. She added, 'I do not know if these are bloodstains. At first, the handkerchief was spotless, very white. Padre Pio used it to dry his hands, and then he gave it to my grandfather Agostino. Over time, very small dots inexplicably appeared. They later expanded, turning into these stains that we can see. This extraordinary event coincided with my grandmother's recovery … but let me explain to you.'

"My Aunt Pia often fainted when she was a child. Nobody could understand the reason. One day, while she was in the countryside with her mother, she fainted and fell on the ground. Grandma Antonia, her mother, immediately invoked Padre Pio.

It happened in the 1940s, and Padre Pio had already left Pietrelcina for San Giovanni Rotondo. But the people of the village still used to pray and ask for his help, because they really believed in his holiness. That was what Grandma Antonia did on that day, keeping her daughter in her arms. She had met Padre Pio when he still lived there, and she remembered him well. She suddenly heard his voice, calling her, 'Antoniè! Antoniè!' She turned around, but she did not see anyone. But in that moment, her daughter woke up. She felt good, and from then on, she never had any health issues. However, something important occurred in her soul. After that, my aunt wanted to become a nun. Her parents left for San Giovanni Rotondo to ask for Padre Pio's opinion. He suggested to wait another year. Pia then became a nun, and she joined the *Preziosissimo Sangue* order, in the monastery of Agnone, near Isernia.

"In 1950, my Grandmother Antonia got sick. She could not breathe because of the pain in her right hip. Several doctors examined her, but they did not find out her disease. Back then, you could not simply go to the ER to get a diagnosis. It was different, especially in our little village, and you had to make do with that. But Grandma's health was worsening, so Grandpa Agostino decided to go to San Giovanni Rotondo to ask for Padre Pio's help.

"When he got there, he was disappointed. Padre Pio was busy with spiritual exercises, and he could not see anyone. Grandpa Agostino was overcome. The journey and his concerns for his wife exhausted him. He sat on a pew in the church, and he burst into tears. A friar noticed him and approached him. My grandfather told him that he had come to see Padre Pio because he really needed his help. That friar put his hand in his pocket, and he took a handkerchief out. He gave it to my grandfather, and he said, 'After Mass, Padre Pio will go back to the sacristy. Give him this handkerchief so that he can dry his hands. Then keep it because it will be an important relic.'

"My grandfather was a little reassured, and he was ready to do what he had been told. Time went by. After Mass, Padre Pio walked among the crowd that was waiting for him. So many people were calling him, reaching out their hands, trying to touch his tunic. My grandfather was among them, intimidated, holding the handkerchief in his hand. At some point, while Padre Pio was walking, he suddenly turned to him. He smiled at him because he was from his same town, and he had already been to San Giovanni. He looked at him deeply, and he said, 'Agostì, tell your wife to change her doctor! And tell her I am praying for her.'

"Grandpa Agostino was stunned; he could not believe it. How could Padre Pio know the reason of his visit to San Giovanni Rotondo? Was he aware that his wife was sick? Then he remembered the handkerchief, and he quickly gave it to Padre Pio. He took it, he dried his hands, and he gave it back to him, smiling again. When he was back home, my grandfather gave the handkerchief to his wife: 'Padre Pio held it in his hands.' And he added, 'He suggests that you change your doctor, and he says he will pray for you.' They decided to follow his advice, so they went to the doctor of the monastery of Agnone, where their daughter Pia was. That doctor examined Gandma Antonia, and he soon diagnosed her with severe appendicitis, which was about to turn into peritonitis. Grandma had emergency surgery, and she was saved. Grandpa Agostino went back to Padre Pio to thank him, but he did not even let him speak. When he saw him, he said, 'Be quiet, Agostì! Do not worry!'

"Grandma Antonia recovered perfectly, and she always kept that handkerchief as a precious relic. Sometimes she grabbed it, to kiss it and pray. One day, she noticed that there were some little red dots on the fabric. As days went by, those dots turned into bigger stains. They looked like the ones that Padre Pio's stigmata left on the bandages, as shown in many pictures. Was the one on the handkerchief blood, too? And what did it mean? Was it perhaps one of Padre Pio's special blessings? We have never found out, but my family has always scrupulously kept this handkerchief, like an actual treasure. For us, it is Padre Pio's handkerchief!"

28

Never Far from Him

Enzo Bertani told me, "I arrived in San Giovanni Rotondo in 1950, and I have always been near Padre Pio until his death. He cared about me, and his prayers saved my wife and my son, whose life was at risk."

Enzo Bertani came from the province of Parma. He was one of those people lucky enough to know Padre Pio, to be next to him, and to work with him. He died in 2016, at the age of eighty-eight. For twenty years, he was one of Padre Pio's close coworkers, a sort of personal secretary. For some time, he was also the treasurer at *Casa Sollievo della Sofferenza*, the hospital founded by Padre Pio in 1956.

"Padre Pio relied on me and gave me important tasks," he told me. "When someone pointed out that I was too young, he used to reply, 'I trust Enzo more than myself.' One of my tasks was to reply to the letters that were sent from all over the world to Padre Pio. He never opened them, but he knew what they were about. He held them in his hand, and then he dictated to me what I had to write. When I opened the envelopes, I found out that he was right. It was amazing, and it happened every day, with hundreds of letters.

"I went to San Giovanni Rotondo for the first time in 1950. At that time, I lived in Venezuela with my brother. I had found a job at the Ministry of Agriculture. While I was on vacation in Italy in 1950, my brother asked me to visit Padre Pio. He was kind, but when I told him I was about to go back to South America, he said, 'No, it is not good for you.' I was surprised, and I explained to him that I had a good job there, and I liked it. 'It is not for you,' he said again.

"I was upset. I kept thinking about what he had said, and eventually, I decided to not leave. I found a job in Parma, but every other week, I went to San Giovanni Rotondo. I felt I could not stay away from Padre Pio. But I was not thinking about moving to the Gargano area.

"On Easter 1951, I was still in San Giovanni Rotondo. The owner of the hotel where I was staying asked me if I wanted to become its manager. I immediately declined, but I also talked about it with Padre Pio. He said, 'Go home, quit your job, and come back here.' That time I did not hesitate. It was impossible to refuse to do something that Padre Pio asked for. I did what he had said, and I became the manager of the hotel. One year later, after morning Mass, Padre Pio told me, 'Tomorrow you will start working with me.' And my life next to him began. At first, I was involved in the prayer groups, but then I became his secretary.

"I wanted to create my own family, but every time I started dating a girl, Padre Pio curtly said, 'Forget about it; she is not right for you.' I was very sad. I thought he did not agree with my idea of getting married because he wanted me to become a friar. But I did not believe that was the right choice for me. He used to tell me, as if he could read my mind, 'Do not worry; you will soon meet the right girl for you.' And he was right. Soon after that, I fell in love with Carmelina, who later became my wife. However, I was at first afraid to talk about it with Padre Pio because

I feared he could tell me I was wrong again. One day he said, 'Come on, what do you need to ask me?' I confided in him. He replied, 'Carmelina is the one that God has meant for you!' I was so happy. On October 17, Padre Pio officiated at our wedding. He explained to us that it was the feast of Our Lady of the Rosary as well as the anniversary of his father's death.

"My wife and I wanted to have children, but we were having difficulties. Carmelina was really sad, and one day, while she was confessing to Padre Pio, she burst into tears. He smiled and said, 'Do not worry; you are already two months pregnant.' We immediately went to the hospital to have some tests done, and it was true. We called our first son Pio. When my wife got pregnant again, Padre Pio told us it was a girl. Back then, it was not possible to have an ultrasound done, so we could not find out the gender of the baby in advance. But Padre Pio knew it, and we did have a baby girl, Irene.

"However, there were some complications with the third pregnancy. My wife hemorrhaged, and she was admitted to the hospital. Her Rh factor was negative, which is very rare and dangerous for the fetus. She urgently needed a blood transfusion, but there were no compatible donors. The situation was so serious that Carmelina received Extreme Unction from the chaplain of the hospital. I was hopeless, and I ran to Padre Pio. He commanded me, 'Find Professor Bettini from Rome!' 'Who is he? How can I find him?' I replied. 'I don't know; I don't know him,' Padre Pio said. 'Contact the state education department in Rome. You may mention my name.'

"I did not stop wondering how Padre Pio could know compatible donors. I had learned that an incomprehensible mystery surrounded him. It was late in the evening. I called the state education department, but I was afraid nobody would answer. However, an employee answered the phone, and he gave me the home phone number of the superintendent. I explained the whole situation to him. He called me back twenty minutes later. He told me he had found Mr. Bettini, the teacher whose blood type was compatible with my wife's. He arrived in the middle of the night, and my wife got the transfusion. Her condition was still critical, but Padre Pio told me, 'Do not worry. Carmelina will suffer on earth but not underground.' My wife did survive. We had a baby boy, and we called him Francesco, Padre Pio's name."

29

A Seal on the Soul

"Padre Pio is the most important person I have ever met," said Mrs. Elena Golia. "He has always been a guiding light in my life, and meeting him was a great delight."

Elena Golia lives in Aversa, near Caserta. She was born in 1945. She is married to a surgeon, and they have two children and five grandchildren. She was a nurse, a nursing teacher, and eventually an elementary school teacher. When she was twenty-one years old, she took a course to become a professional nurse at the hospital *Casa Sollievo della Sofferenza* in San Giovanni Rotondo. "I had the chance to spend time with Padre Pio. He was already old and sick. I saw him in the hallway of the monastery: he was in a wheelchair, pushed by one of his brothers. When he looked at me, his eyes were on fire. I still get emotional when I think about those moments that I have never forgotten. Can you believe that the first time I went to Padre Pio for Confession, he brusquely sent me away?"

"The first time I met him, I was sixteen years old, in 1961. I was a restless girl, and I had so many questions and doubts. I was looking for my own path in life. My mother noticed I was suffering and dissatisfied, so she made me visit Padre Pio. My mom was a spiritual daughter of his, and she believed he could give me the right advice. Therefore, I went to San Giovanni Rotondo, but it was not really my choice; I went there to please my mother. But in the confessional, Padre Pio was very harsh with me. He said, 'Get up and leave!' I was really disappointed. I was a regular girl, like many others. I was mad, and I thought, 'Who does he think he is?' but just for a moment. I quickly realized he had reacted like that, not because of my sins, but rather because I was not sure of what I was doing. He could tell I did not really mean it. He was strict because he wanted to rouse people's souls. But in that moment, I felt humiliated. I was about to leave the church when someone called me. It was a friar, telling me to go back to Padre Pio. When I was again in front of him, I bent on my knees, and I kissed his hand. Something I can't explain happened, as if my soul had departed my body. I felt like I was flying, surrounded by an immeasurable peace. I was alert, and I was aware I was on my knees, but at the same time, I felt like I was in the sky.

"From that moment, Padre Pio was part of me. There was a seal on my soul, and I knew I was never going to distance myself from him. Four years later, in 1966, I went back to San Giovanni Rotondo to take a nursing class. I lived in the boarding school of *Casa Sollievo,* a few steps away from the monastery, and it was amazing to live so close to Padre Pio.

"There was a special atmosphere every day. I can say it felt like being in heaven. I remember that the nurses who were studying like me could confess to Padre Pio at prearranged times. However, if a girl did not show up, I quickly took advantage of the situation and spent some time with him. One day, I asked him if he acknowledged me as his spiritual daughter. He told me, 'If you behave, you will be my spiritual daughter.' When he said the words 'my daughter,' I burst into tears because I was so happy. It was the best reward for me. Sometimes I asked for his advice about my future as a nurse and the classes I should take. He fatherly supported me: 'Yes, I think you should do it!'

"In that spiritual climate, I wondered if I should become a nun. I was seriously thinking about it, and I told Padre Pio about it. 'You will create your own holy family,' he said. I was curious and a little naive, so I asked him, 'Father, are you going to introduce to me the man I will marry?' He was serious, and replied: 'It is not the right time yet.' Years later I went back home, and I started working at the hospital. There I met a surgery resident who later became my husband.

"I remember that one day I was waiting for Padre Pio in the hallway of the old church. I was with another student. Padre Pio was in a wheelchair, pushed by one of his brothers. I was staring at him, and I was thrilled as always when I was around him. He passed by without saying anything, but after a few meters, he told his brother to stop. He came back to me, stretched out his hand, and gently touched my forehead with the forefinger of his right hand. It was a simple gesture, but I had no idea there was something special about it. I found out its meaning only a few years later, while I was reading a book. It said that Padre Pio had told one of his brothers, 'My whole strength is held in my right hand.' He had touched me with that finger, giving me the best blessing.

"I have another very moving memory, which dates back to Lent 1967. Lent represented a very unique time for Padre Pio. During each Mass, he concretely and physically lived through the sufferings of Jesus' passion again. During Lent, however, the pain was even more intense. On that occasion, the nun took us, the students, to watch Padre Pio from the hallway between the sacristy and the cloistered convent. He passed by in front of us: he was melancholy and bowed. He looked exhausted. The nun told him, 'Father, say something to the girls.' He turned around and looked at us. He was pale and tired. 'Do not make me talk,' he whispered. 'I can't even speak!' I realized then that the pain Padre Pio felt because of the stigmata was really intense.

"I also remember when he died, on September 23, 1968. I had seen him praying in the church the day before, and I was excited because the next day he was going to hear my confession. I went downstairs in the crypt that had recently been built. The place where Padre Pio would have been buried had already been selected, but nobody could have thought it was going to happen a few hours later. I had a sort of premonition. The block of marble where Padre Pio's remains were going to be kept was in the middle of the crypt. A crucifix was on top of it. I thought, 'Jesus is on Padre Pio's grave. It means he will die soon.' I quickly stopped thinking about it, and I told myself that Padre Pio was still going to be with us for a long time. That night, however, a persistent buzz woke me up. There were people standing in front of the church, and their voices were sad and worried. Then some nurses came and told us, 'Padre Pio has died!' I thought it was a terrible joke. We ran to the monastery, and we found out it was true. I was upset, but at the same time, I was happy to know he was finally in heaven. And from up there, he has always been with me. Sometimes I am not aware of it, but I know he takes care of me, and he helps me with my everyday life."

30

The Spiritual Children's Needs

Lucia Centra is eighty-two years old. She lives in Perugia, but she was born in San Giovanni Rotondo. Padre Pio officiated at her wedding. She told me, "He celebrated my wedding on April 2, 1964. It was an unforgettable event, one that I had really wished for. For all of us from the village, Padre Pio was the friar who did miracles, but he was also a loving father who helped you during your everyday life. People asked him advice for all sorts of things. That was what he wanted. He really cared about the needs of his spiritual children, and he often took care of them in a special way, like a saint.

"I was a child when I met Padre Pio. He was there when I received my First Communion. I attended catechism with other children. Our teacher was Mary Pyle, a wealthy lady from New Jersey. She had met Padre Pio in 1923, and after that, she had never left San Giovanni Rotondo. They used to call her 'the American lady.' We often went to the monastery, we attended Mass celebrated by Padre Pio, and we joined the processions. We were used to seeing Padre Pio every day.

"I remember that once, he reprimanded me for wearing a dress he believed to be too short. The hem of the skirt was slightly above the knees, and he did not like it. He always paid attention to how women dressed. He was not narrow-minded, but he was rather worried that fashion could affect women's dignity. I was sixteen or seventeen years old, but I remember it like it was yesterday. After Confession, it was common to move the little curtain aside and kiss his hand. That was what I did, and then I was about to walk away. But suddenly, he called me. I heard 'Psss! Psss!' I turned around, and Padre Pio was signaling me to go back to him. I got closer, and he said aloud, so that everybody could hear him, 'Today I absolve you, but if next time you come dressed like this again, I will send you away!' I blushed hard.

"In 1964, Giovanni (my future husband) and I decided to get married. My dream was that Padre Pio celebrate our wedding; it was really important to me. I had found out that since he was often sick, in order for Padre Pio to celebrate the wedding, we needed to get an authorization from the superior of the province. Giovanni visited then the Capuchin monks in Foggia. A friar, who was the custodian, sent him to a specific office. There, however, Giovanni was told it was impossible: Padre Pio's health condition was too unstable, so they were no longer issuing authorizations. I was very disappointed.

"The following day, during my confession, I confided it to him. 'Father, there is something that makes me really sad,' I said. 'What happened?' he asked me. 'I am getting married on April 2. I was really hoping you could celebrate the wedding. It is my biggest wish.' 'And why is it not possible?' I explained to him then that my fiancé had gone to Foggia, but he had not been given the authorization. 'Tell him to go there again!' he replied. I told him I doubted that Giovanni would accept to go back since the first time it had been unsuccessful. 'And I have told you to send him again!' he shouted, so loudly that the whole church probably heard him.

"As I expected, Giovanni refused to go back to Foggia. However, I told him that if he didn't go, I would not marry him. So he went back to Foggia, and the custodian sent him to the same office. He walked in and asked if Padre Pio could celebrate our wedding on April 2. That time, surprisingly, they let him sit. He waited a few minutes, and he eventually got the authorization. I am not sure how he did it, but Padre Pio probably had dealt with it.

"Padre Pio was always close to my family. Somehow he even helped my father with his job. After the war, my dad was the manager of a large farm. He was responsible for the amount of wheat that they had to consign to the State. That year, however, the owner of the farm did not pay the farmers with money but, rather, with wheat. Eventually, there was something wrong, and it was a mess. My father was reported because he was the manager, and they even wanted to put him in prison. My mother hid him then in the attic so that the police could not find him. He used to leave the attic only at night to spend time with us. One early morning, my dad wanted to confess to Padre Pio. My mother was worried because he could have been noticed, but he walked through the fields and got to the monastery. He managed to confess, and at the end, he said he was hoping to walk through the main street of the village. Padre Pio said, 'No! Follow the same route, as you did earlier.' In was clear that Padre Pio knew that my dad had secretly traveled to the monastery. He also knew that my father was innocent, and that it was better if he kept hiding for some time. The denunciation was eventually withdrawn, and my dad was absolved.

"After this episode however, my father was unemployed. He had to take care of the family, but because of a childhood disease in one of his arms, he was not fit for strenuous work. When he was younger, he had worked as a shoemaker, so he opted for that job. But my mother had doubts. She kept saying, 'Who will come to your shop? You have not worked as a shoemaker for a long time.' My mom also shared her concerns with Padre Pio, but he replied, 'That is the right job for him!'

"One night, my mother had a dream about Padre Pio. He was holding a sandal in his hand and told her, 'Go to your husband, and have it fixed!' It was the message she had been waiting for. From that moment, she supported her husband's decision, and he became a successful shoemaker. He made a good amount of money. In a week, he earned what my husband (a police officer) used to earn in a month. He bought a new house, and he helped me with my wedding. We owe everything to our beloved Padre Pio!"

31

"This Is the Friar I See!"

In the province of Vibo Valentia, in Drapia, an amazing and unique facility is being built. It is Padre Pio's *Cittadella*. It is a huge building that includes a sanctuary, a children's hospital, a research center, and a village for the patients. Everything looks exactly like Padre Pio wanted it to be, as he had asked of his spiritual daughter, Irene Gaeta.

This kind lady is eighty-three years old and has a sweet smile. Padre Pio has been visiting her for more than sixty years. She used to see him when he was alive, and after his death, she sees him in her dreams and in her visions. Padre Pio gives her advice, he helps her, and he gives her instructions on how to build facilities to help others. When I met her, she told me, "I can see Padre Pio as clearly as I see you right now. He is always very categorical: when there is something he cares about, it needs to be done. You have no choice!"

Everything about Irene Gaeta may sound illogical or imaginary. What is real, however, are the results—that is, the aid facilities that have been created for those in need, thanks to Padre Pio's advice. Church leaders have also liked these initiatives, and they support them. Following Padre Pio's specific instructions, Irene has founded community homes in Italy and abroad for poor and sick people and for single mothers. In Sestriere, on top of Mount Fraiteve, a chapel has been built. Several statues of Padre Pio were erected in different Italian squares. In Vitinia, in the Roman suburbs, the *Cittadella di Padre Pio* has been built, which includes a new parish and a new church. She also founded the secular organization *I Discepoli di Padre Pio* (The Disciples of Padre Pio), acknowledged by the Holy See, whose goal is to help those in need. The association has its own rules that were put into writing by Gerardo di Flumeri, as Padre Pio wanted. Di Flumeri was the one who took care of Padre Pio's process for beatification. Mrs. Irene and the *Discepoli* have already founded many community homes in Italy and abroad, such as in Argentina, Sri Lanka, Canada, and the United States. They organize pilgrimages and prayers that are always attended by many people.

Irene told me, "I am just an instrument of heaven. It all began in 1946 when I was nine years old. One evening, I saw a friar standing next to my bed. He told me he was Padre Pio from Pietrelcina. He explained to me that, the following day, my father was going to get an important letter. My dad was responsible for the gardens of the Quirinale Palace. However, after the referendum of 1946, the king was exiled, and my father lost his job. He did not know how to provide for his family. But the letter that Padre Pio had mentioned arrived. Because of his large family and his merits, he was offered a job in the Forestry Corps.

"During those years, Padre Pio often visited me. I had never heard about him, and I thought he was a saint from the past, rather than a living friar. One day, I saw a picture of him in the newspaper. 'This is the friar I see!' I shouted. I immediately decided to visit him in San Giovanni Rotondo. I remember the first time we met as if it were yesterday. Padre Pio soon entrusted me with a mission. He said it was a mission that the Virgin Mary was entrusting me with. I was supposed to take home to Frosinone a friend of mine. I had not understood very well the reason behind that task. That same night, while I was in the hotel, Padre Pio appeared to me, explaining again what I had to do. My friend's father was about to die, and during his prayers, he had asked the Virgin Mary to see again his daughter, because she had been missing from home for ten years. I took her to him so that when the man passed away, he was finally at peace.

"In 1961, Padre Pio appeared again to me. He told me I was going to come into contact with the Roman aristocracy, in order to help those that had forgotten about God. I was a seamstress. Soon after that, I opened a fashion house on Frattina Street. Some of the most well-known people in Rome were my customers, just like Padre Pio had said. I helped many of them to rediscover the meaning of compassion. One day, Padre Pio appeared to me while he was celebrating Mass, wearing the holy vestments. But he was not holding the goblet in his hand. 'Bring it to me!' he told me. I said I did not have the money necessary to buy a goblet for Mass, but he replied that I was going to find it in three days. Soon after that, the famous actress Alida Chelli called me. She ordered eleven dresses, and she told me she needed them within the next three days. She paid me, so I was able to take a goblet to San Giovanni Rotondo. When he saw me, he said, 'Dear girl, you are finally here!'

"Padre Pio then wanted me to begin a nonprofit association of his spiritual children that could help those in need. It was October 1999. Padre Pio had been beatified five months earlier. He appeared to me and said, 'Dear girl, gather a group of people that believe in the gospel like I did!' Wow! That was really an important task. I talked about it with Fr. Gerardo di Flumeri, who had dealt with Padre Pio's beatification, and he chose the name 'Disciples of Padre Pio.' The association needed to have its own rules, therefore, following Padre Pio's advice, and I asked Fr. Gerardo to write them. But he refused because he was already seriously ill, and he had little time left to live. One morning, around 5:00 am, I saw Padre Pio in my room. I immediately asked him to intercede for Fr. Gerardo. He closed his eyes, as if he were praying. Then he said, 'Done. Now you can tell him to write down the rules.' In that exact moment, Fr. Gerardo woke up, completely healed. He wrote the rules of the association, and he lived for another ten years."

32

Padre Pio's Sugared Almonds

"Padre Pio died on the night of September 23, 1968. My father was a health worker in San Giovanni Rotondo, and the friars of the monastery called him to attest to the death and to prepare the corpse for the burial. It was a very difficult moment for my dad. Padre Pio was his mentor, a friend, the one who wanted him to be a doctor in San Giovanni. But it was also an intense spiritual moment because, my father said, he was touching the body of a saint. He touched his hair and brushed his beard tenderly, surrounded by the strong flower scent that Padre Pio emanated, even after he had died."

This is what Luisella Grifa told me. She is forty-seven years old, and she is a lawyer in San Giovanni Rotondo. Dr. Giovanni Grifa was her father, a very beloved man in the village. He died in 2016, but people still remember him as a unique doctor, kind and helpful.

"He was a sweet man, but at the same time, he was very strict at work. There were nine people in my family: my father, my mom, my six siblings, and I. Dad loved telling us that, somehow, he was similar to Padre Pio: loving but also authoritarian. We grew up with vitamins, books, and prayers. He basically lived in obscurity. He was born in 1929, so at that time, Padre Pio had been in San Giovanni Rotondo for thirteen years, and people already believed he was a saint.

"When he was a child, my dad often went to the monastery. One of his older sisters, Filomena, was one of Padre Pio's spiritual daughters, and when she visited him, she always took her little brother with her. Dad used to tell me that when he was close to that friar, he felt safe, protected, and loved. Then he told me about the sugared almonds that Padre Pio gave him. This is something that not everyone knows about. Padre Pio loved giving sugared almonds to children, the white ones with an almond inside. They were the typical ones that are used at weddings and First Communions. They were pretty rare back then, but he always kept a few of them in the pocket of his tunic for the children who visited him.

"My dad attended medical school in Cagliari. He graduated in 1957, and he wanted to continue living there because he had met my mom, who was Sardinian. But Padre Pio made him change his mind. Among the citizens of San Giovanni Rotondo, it was common to visit Padre Pio and to ask for his advice, even if it dealt with daily life. My father then shared with him his doubts and mentioned the possibility of becoming a doctor and starting a family in Sardinia. But Padre Pio replied, 'There are not enough doctors in San Giovanni!' My father did not need to hear anything more. With his observation, Padre Pio wanted to express his wish to be close to that man he had known for so long. But also, he was already aware that my dad was going to help several people in the village. Perhaps he even knew that my father would be the last one to say goodbye to him.

"Because of his job, Dad was asked to confirm Padre Pio's death. He was one of the first ones to see him after he had passed away. He used to tell me about the phone call he got, in the middle of the night, and the rush to the monastery. Then he gently followed the health procedure to prepare the corpse for the burial. When he remembered those moments, my dad kept mentioning how emotional he got when he touched Padre Pio. He was almost hesitant. He managed to caress his face because he felt the urgency to touch him one last time. He carefully brushed his beard, and some hair got stuck in the comb. Dad kept the hair as a precious relic. He also kept the veil he had spread out on Padre Pio's face and a piece of sealing wax used to seal the coffin. Later, together with other doctors and friends of Padre Pio, he had taken the coffin on his shoulders and moved it from the cell where the friar had died to the church.

"My father also told me about Padre Pio's stigmata. While he was examining the corpse, in order to confirm the death, he had the chance to see Padre Pio's hands, feet, and ribs. The skin was clean, intact, perfect. There was no evidence of the bloody wounds that Padre Pio had had for fifty years in a row. Those sores were not a secret, since everybody had seen the ones on his hands when he took off his gloves during Mass. That night, my father noticed that those open and bloody wounds had disappeared, without leaving any trace. He was fascinated because it was something that science could not explain, and you could only believe it if you had faith.

"Padre Pio's funeral took place three days after his death, on September 26. My dad said that, even though three days had gone by, Padre Pio's body was still releasing a strong flower scent. It was the same fragrance that his stigmata emanated when he was alive and that all his spiritual children had smelled. But there is something more I want to tell you. It is an episode that really moved my father. When I was born, some complications occurred. I spent a month in the incubator because my life was constantly in danger. During that time, my dad went back and forth between the hospital where I was, *Casa Sollievo*, and Padre Pio's grave, which, back then, was still located in the crypt of the little church *Santa Maria delle Grazie*. In his prayers, he asked his friend to watch over me, and after thirty days, something happened. While he was in front of Padre Pio's grave, my father sensed something, a sort of answer to his prayers. We never found out about the details, whether he had seen or heard something. But we know that he immediately took me out of the incubator, and we went home. The doctors at the hospital did not agree, and they tried to change his mind. They said it was dangerous, but he was determined. He took me home, and I quickly began recovering."

33

"You Made Me Look Ugly!"

Michele Miglionico, from Taranto, is a painter and a sculptor, and he is internationally famous. He is the only one that created a funeral portrayal of Padre Pio, a few hours after his death. He was born in San Giovanni Rotondo, so his memories about Padre Pio date back to his childhood.

"I met him when I was a child," he told me. "He encouraged me to become an artist. I was one of the first people to see him after his death. That was when I made a portrait of his face. And the story behind that portrait is amazing.

"I often visited Padre Pio. It was a common habit: moms took their children with them to the monastery, to get his blessing. A lot of people always wanted to see him. We used to wait for him in the hallway, between the monastery and the sacristy of the little church *Santa Maria delle Grazie*. There was a barrier there, to prevent people from swarming in the hallway. But other children and I managed to slip away, and we approached Padre Pio. He touched us, and sometimes he gave us a candy and a little slap on the head, which was his way of blessing the little ones.

"When I was six or seven years old, I was the altar boy in a church of the village, near my house. We need to keep in mind, indeed, that not everyone could attend Padre Pio's Mass because the monastery was kilometers away from the village. I was the altar boy during the Mass celebrated by Fr. Salvatore Novelli. He was one of the few priests in San Giovanni Rotondo that had publicly supported Padre Pio in the 1930s, while all the other ones went against him. He was a brave man. Back then, it was dangerous for a priest to defend Padre Pio because the Vatican had already condemned him once. It was Fr. Salvatore's idea to send me to Padre Pio to serve at Mass. One day, he told my mother about it, and she agreed. She took me to the monastery, and Padre Pio was happy: he always was when he was surrounded by children. He reminded me of a caring grandfather, but he was also strict when it was necessary.

"I remember well all the times I was excited, next to him on the altar. On those occasions, I could clearly see the wounds on his hands because during the Consecration, he used to take off the gloves that hid them. One morning, in May, Padre Pio was celebrating Mass outside, under one of the porches of the monastery. I remember perfectly that a ray of sunshine passed through his hand. That was exactly what happened: the light passed through his wound. I realized, therefore, that Padre Pio's sores were actual holes, which passed through the palms, from one side to the other.

"On another occasion, I was putting the sacred objects back in the sacristy. I ended up holding the corporal in my hands. The corporal is the linen cloth that the priest lays out on the altar, and then he places the goblet on it. I am ashamed to admit it, but I put it in my pocket. I took it away with me, and I still have it. I know it was not a good deed, but Padre Pio did not say anything about it. He always knew everything, and if he did not scold me, there was clearly a reason. I have been devoutly keeping that linen for my whole life. Every time I remember he used it during the Mass, I get very emotional.

"When I was young, I helped my uncle in San Giovanni Rotondo. He was the owner of a public transportation company. I was the ticket collector on the bus that took the people from the village to the monks. Every day, I saw many pilgrims that went to the monastery to meet Padre Pio. I remember several famous people. For example, for actor Carlo Campanini, the monastery was his second home. There were also Macario; Tina Pica, the great actress; Princess Beatrice di Savoia; Elettra Marconi, the daughter of the Nobel Prize winner Guglielmo Marconi; and even Rachele Mussolini, the Duce's wife.

"In the 1950s, my father emigrated to Paris for work. The rest of the family joined him, and we lived there for a few years. I decided to become an artist in that beautiful city, after staring, fascinated, at the painters in Montmartre. When I came back to San Giovanni, my middle school teacher was Francesco Paolo Fiorentino. He was a painter, a poet, and a comedy writer, and he was also one of Padre Pio's spiritual sons. He noticed I had a talent for drawing, so one day, at church, he told me, 'Go make a portrait of Padre Pio!' I grabbed a piece of plywood, a charcoal pencil, and I got closer to the friar that was praying. I depicted him, and then I showed the drawing to the professor. He encouraged me to show it to Padre Pio as well. I was a little intimidated, but Fiorentino came with me. 'Father,' he said, 'look what Michele just did.' Padre Pio observed the drawing, he became serious, and then he made a beautiful smile. 'Man, I look so ugly!' he said. But he was laughing, and he touched my head. I am sure he knew I was going to devote my life to art, and that was his way of telling me he agreed. A few years later, I moved to Paris to study art.

"I was twenty-two years old when Padre Pio died. I was a young artist. I had recently finished my studies at the French academy, and people in my field had begun acknowledging me. I knew the friars well, and the day after Padre Pio's death, they asked me to go to the monastery together with Fiorentino. They wanted a portrait of his face before moving him to the crypt. It was supposed to be used for the cast of the death mask, which, however, was never made. We were very emotional. Professor Fiorentino was so moved that the pencil fell out of his hands. He could not keep working, so he asked me to continue with the work. I probably should not say it because I am its author, but it is a beautiful portrait. Padre Pio's face is so peaceful that it is impossible to describe it. He looks asleep, completely at peace.

"I kept that drawing for many years, until 1974. At that time, I was living in Taranto, and I had planned an art exhibition at a gallery in the city. I displayed all the drawings I had made in the streets of Paris and also the funeral portrayal of Padre Pio. At some point, an elegant lady walked in the gallery. She was interested in my drawings. When she ended up in front of Padre Pio's portrait, she did not move for a while. She was bowled over. Then she told me she wanted to buy it, and she asked me the price. I did not want to sell it because I was fond of it. However, I did not want to be rude by starkly saying no to her. So I opted for a huge price for that time: 450,000 lire. She did not bat an eyelid. She took a checkbook out of her purse, and she paid me. Then, she took the drawing and left.

"Years later, I was surprised to find out that the lady was the countess Concetta Lanfranchi. She was the president of the women's branch of the political association *Unione Monarchica Italiana*. She had bought the portrait to give it to Umberto di Savoia, who was a spiritual son of Padre Pio. Umberto jealously kept it as a relic, and before dying, he gave it to the deputy Luigi Filippo

Benedettini, who was then the president of *Unione Monarchica*. For several years, the portrait had been displayed in the headquarters of the association, in Rome. It was only recently that Benedettini's heirs brought it back to San Giovanni Rotondo. It can now be found in the chapel of *Casa Sollievo della Sofferenza*. There is no better place for it than in the hospital that Padre Pio had so long dreamed about."

34

The Last Goodbye

I met Leandro Carboncini in 2016. I had visited him in Dalmine, near Bergamo, where he lived with his wife, Valeria, in a house surrounded by greenery. He died in February 2020. He was born in 1924, and he was a former employee at the steelworks in Dalmine. He was a very kind person, and I remember his story about his friendship with Padre Pio.

"I met him in 1950, and he immediately turned into my second guardian angel," he told me. "Padre Pio was very sweet and caring. He took care of all his spiritual children, and his fatherly tenderness was moving. Thanks to him, I recovered from a lung disease, I found a job, and I even got married. I spent time with him until his death, and I have great memories. I really owe him a lot.

"Everything started with a letter. When I was twenty-six years old, I got sick with bronchial pneumonia, which later turned into an apical pulmonary infiltration. Back then, I lived in Viareggio, where I was born, and I worked at the Picchiotti shipyard. However, because of my health condition, which forced me to stay in bed for months, I eventually lost my job. My condition was so serious that the doctors attempted to treat me with an innovative treatment, Streptomycin, which had recently been discovered in the United States. But rather than feeling better, I was getting weaker.

"The first person who told me about Padre Pio was one of my mother's friends. She gave me a book written by Dr. Giorgio Festa, who was one of the first doctors that had examined Padre Pio's stigmata. I read it, and I found out about all the amazing events that were taking place thanks to this friar from Gargano: the healings, bilocation, and the passion marks on his body. I was very impressed, so I decided to write him a letter, and I entrusted my health to his prayers. Besides, I promised him that if I recovered, I would visit him to thank him in person.

"One night, I felt someone tenderly stroking my cheek. I woke up, and I thought it was my mom sitting next to me, but there was no one. I was immediately surrounded by a strong rose fragrance. I had often heard about Padre Pio's mysterious scents, so I realized I was going to recover soon. I quickly began to improve, and two months later, I was on my way to San Giovanni Rotondo.

"I remember very well my first meeting with Padre Pio. The only way to talk to him was to go to Confession. There were always many people. You had to book in advance and wait for your turn, but the wait could last for days. I was scared because some people used to say he was unsociable and ill-tempered and that sometimes he rudely sent people away. I was intimidated. I had prepared a list of my sins, and I kept repeating it, in order to be ready. When it was my turn, my legs were shaking, but Padre Pio was very sweet. He stroked my cheek, and he did not even let me talk: he listed all my sins in the same order I had planned. I was shocked. He absolved me, and he smiled at me. I told him, 'Father, I was sick, but I recovered. I came here to thank you.' He put his hand on my head and replied, 'Let's thank God then!'

"From that moment, I started visiting him at least once a year. I considered him a father figure to whom I could ask for help when I needed. For example, I had recovered, but I still did not have a job. I talked to him about it, and he said he was going to pray for me. Soon after that, the Dalmine company hired me, and I worked for them for thirty-two years. Once I had a job, I asked for his help because I really wanted to create my own family. A few months went by, and I met Valeria; we were married on November 21, 1959. During our honeymoon, we went to Rome and Viareggio, and then we eventually went to San Giovanni Rotondo because I wanted to introduce her to Padre Pio. He blessed us, and then he gave us some tender little slaps on our heads: one to me and two for Valeria! She has a livelier personality than me, and Padre Pio definitely knew it!

"My wife and I often visited him. I remember a particular episode. On our way back home, we were traveling along the road that goes below the monastery. When we managed to see the window of Padre Pio's cell, we waved at him, and we quietly asked him to accompany us during our journey. We suddenly smelled an intense fragrance: it was his reply to our greeting. Another time, he played a joke on Valeria. He was strict when it came to women's clothing: women's skirts had to cover the knee. At times, he had sent some ladies away because he thought their skirts were too short. My wife had bought a new one: it did cover the knee but maybe not enough. Padre Pio probably did not like it. During Mass, when Valeria moved closer to the altar to receive Communion, she noticed that the hem of the skirt had been completely and perfectly unsewed so that the skirt was longer. But it was new and intact when my wife had worn it! We understood then that Padre Pio did not approve.

"He had a playful personality, and his jokes were hilarious. I remember that once, we were in the vegetable garden of the monastery, together with some bishops. Padre Pio said, 'I am going to tell you a saying that belongs to the medical school of Salerno: a sick person between two doctors is like a cat between two dogs!' We all laughed. Another time, the actor Carlo Campanini, who was very close to Padre Pio, was there. During Mass, while he was singing '*Al ciel, al ciel andrò a vederla un dì . . .*' ('To Heaven, to Heaven I will go to see her one day . . .'), Campanini hit the wrong note, and Padre Pio noticed that. Later, in the sacristy, while he was taking off his vestment, Padre Pio looked at Campanini, and said, 'Oh yes, it is hard to climb up to heaven!'

"On September 23, 1968, Padre Pio died. I heard the news while I was in Viareggio. I took the whole family to Dalmine, and I immediately left for San Giovanni Rotondo with some friends. People from everywhere were coming for the funeral, which took place three days later. More than one hundred thousand people were there. It was really sad, but we knew that Padre Pio was always going to watch over us because he had promised us on several occasions. That same night, my friends and I decided to go back home. We often stopped while driving. During one of these stops, we parked in an area where there was a garage. The headlights of the car were lighting the glass window, when we suddenly saw Padre Pio's unmistakable outline. It was there, on that opaque glass. We were all touched, so we started praying, crying. The image kept being visible for the whole time, until we left. Padre Pio had wanted to say goodbye one last time."

35

"Jesus Wants You to Be a Priest."

Fraternità Francescana di Betania (the Franciscan Fraternity of Bethany) is a one-of-a-kind religious institute. It is the first mixed institute in Church history—that is, made up of both men and women that live and pray together. It was established by Fr. Pancrazio (Nicola Gaudioso), who was one of Padre Pio's spiritual sons. Monsignor Tonino Bello acknowledged the Fraternity as a public association of worshippers in 1987, and in 1998, it was recognized as an institute of consecrated life, of diocesan law. Nowadays, it is in Italy, but it can also be found in Switzerland, Germany, and Brazil.

Fr. Pancrazio met Padre Pio in 1950. It all started after that meeting. It was Fr. Pancrazio who told me about it. I had visited him in Terlizzi, in the motherhouse, soon before his death in 2016, when he was ninety years old.

"I owe Padre Pio everything," he told me. "He suggested what to do with my life. He knew what my future was going to be like, and his words were determinant and prophetic for me. This religious institute was established because of him. He believed in it, and I am sure he is still taking care of it from heaven."

Fr. Pancrazio became a Capuchin monk in 1942—"a lay monk," he explained to me. "It means I was not a priest. I was not good at studying theology, which was necessary for priesthood. I had tried, but I just could not do it. My superiors had sent me to Loreto, to take care of the Holy House in the *Santuario della Santa Casa*. I used to welcome the pilgrims, and I had also founded a prayer group in the name of Padre Pio. Day by day, the group was growing, so I began worrying. I thought I was not going to be able to handle all those people who kept asking for advice for their spiritual journeys. I decided, therefore, to visit Padre Pio in person, and to ask for his advice.

"It was 1950. I went to Confession, and then Padre Pio explained to me the importance of the little things. I remember he explained to me how all of us, in our lives, can aim for holiness. Holiness does not mean doing amazing things, but it rather means carrying out ordinary tasks amazingly well. It was a great lesson: it helped me study in depth St. Francis's life and the mystery of the Holy Family.

"Throughout the years, I often visited Padre Pio. In 1959, I asked him, 'Father, since you can see my future, can you tell me more about my life?' He then gave me a piece of paper, where he had written his suggestion for me. It was a sentence that referred to Bethany, where Lazarus and his sisters, Martha and Mary, lived. According to the Gospel, Jesus used to go to Bethany to rest and pray. He stayed with these friends of his. Martha was always busy, trying to welcome Jesus and his apostles appropriately. She complained because her sister, Mary, was instead always next to Jesus, listening to him. In that piece of paper, Padre Pio had written: 'Do not be so busy as Martha as to forget about Mary's silence. May the Virgin Mary be a kind role model and an inspiration for you. She is very good at reconciling both activities.'

"In that moment, I did not understand what he was trying to tell me, but later, after his death, it was all clear to me. Padre Pio was suggesting that I follow the example of the Virgin Mary, who was both as busy as Martha and as silent as Mary. He was telling me, then, to live a religious life, focusing both on good deeds and prayers.

"I saw Padre Pio for the last time in 1968, a few weeks before his death. He was not feeling well, and I didn't want to bother him. But then, I took courage, and I got closer to him. I confessed to him, and in the end, he told me, 'Jesus wants you to be a priest. It is up to you. Make sure to respect God's will.' Those were strange words: I was puzzled. I was not expecting such a suggestion. I was already forty-two years old, and I did not think I could go back to study to become a priest. But I kept thinking about Padre Pio's words, even after his death. I mentioned it to my superiors, and when they heard what Padre Pio's advice was, they were puzzled as well. They told me, 'It is your decision.'

"I then visited another great mystic that I knew, Mother Speranza. She was a famous Spanish mystic who lived in Collevalenza, near Perugia. I asked her what she thought about Padre Pio's advice. Without any hesitation, she replied, 'Jesus told me the same thing; he wants you to be a priest.' At that moment, I could not refuse. I went back to my books, and I studied theology for four years. It was very hard, but every time I took an exam, I felt like someone was next to me, helping me. I finished my studies, and I became a priest.

"I kept focusing on the prayer group of Loreto, but after a while, I realized God was telling me to lead a new sort of religious life: a life similar to the one of the first Christian communities, similar to *Casa di Betania* (Bethany House). Suddenly, I remembered Padre Pio's note. He had not merely told me how to lead my religious life, but he had also intentionally referred to Bethany. He had basically provided me with the spiritual guidelines of my project. The idea was that of a religious institute that could remind people of a family. Male and female believers that live in the same place, as a big family, like Bethany House and the first Christian communities. The Acts of the Apostles explain how the Church was born. Once Jesus was in heaven, his disciples went back to Jerusalem. In the Acts, we read, 'When they entered the city they went to the upper room where they were staying, Peter and John and James and Andrew, Philip and Thomas, Bartholomew and Matthew, James son of Alphaeus, Simon the Zealot, and Judas son of James. All these devoted themselves with one accord to prayer, together with some women, and Mary the mother of Jesus, and his brothers' (Acts 1:13-14). That was the origin of the Church: the apostles, a few women, and Mary. The first Christian communities included all the representatives of the population. And I realized that it was what God wanted me to do.

"My job was to focus on hospitality. It meant to provide a home to those who needed to rest their souls, to meditate, to think, to change their lives, so that they could find their place. We are here, and we welcome whoever wants to join us. We do not welcome our visitors coldly, accommodating them in a building next to our monastery. We accommodate them 'inside' the monastery. Those who come here live with us, pray with us, eat with us, and talk to us. They are involved in our life here. It was a new idea, somehow even revolutionary. I realized it was exactly what Padre Pio had suggested to me."

36

"Everything Will Be Alright."

Professor Raffaele Augello told me, "When Padre Pio found out that I studied languages, he said, laughing, 'You are then a *linguacciuto* (loudmouth)!' I was disappointed at first, but that was just the way he was: affectionate, facetious, and cheerful. The last time I saw him was a month before his death. That time, he blessed me, and I never forgot it."

Professor Augello was born in 1937, and he has a degree in languages and literature. He is the author of several books on Padre Pio, and he is a point of reference in San Giovanni Rotondo when it comes to the friar's story because he has done much research.

"I was born in this village, and I have always been devoted to Padre Pio. My family was always very grateful to him. My parents lost a son, when he was twenty-one years old, to bronchial pneumonia. When Michele, another son, got sick with the same disease, they turned to Padre Pio. They did not explicitly ask for his recovery. They had faith in his prayers, and they asked him if they could use one of the ambulances that had recently become available in the village. The ambulances were necessary for the health center that was about to be opened. It was 1949. Thanks to that ambulance, my brother was quickly taken to the hospital in Foggia, and he survived. Miracles are not always phenomenal recoveries, but they can also be 'coincidences.' The ambulance was available because Padre Pio had wanted it to be there, and thanks to it, Michele managed to survive. For this reason, my parents owed him a lot.

"When I was twelve years old, my dad took me to Padre Pio for my confession. I remember that his charisma intimidated me a little. He absolved me, and he solemnly said, 'Do not do it again!' Now, I do not remember what my sins were, but I believe it was not anything serious. I had just received my First Communion; I was just a kid. But still, his words had an impact on me, as well as his sign of the cross, marked so seriously and strongly on my head.

"In 1959, I started working for the railroad in Milan. It was also my junior year in college, and I was about to take a very important exam. I got sick with acute appendicitis, and I urgently needed surgery because I was at risk for peritonitis. But I had to take the exam, so I decided to ask Padre Pio for advice. My former professor of philosophy, Vincenzo Mercurio, was devoted to him, and he was the one who took me to him. 'Father, this is Raffaele, one of my former students. Now he is studying languages at college.' he explained to him. Padre Pio laughed, 'Ah, you are a loudmouth then!' I told him about my problem, and he replied, 'You can go to take the exam. After that, go to the hospital. Everything will be fine.' He was right. I easily took the exam, and then I went to the hospital to have surgery.

"I also remember when I had to take the German exam. The professor found out that I was from San Giovanni Rotondo. 'Padre Pio's village!' he said. 'Is it true that he does miracles?' I explained to him that I had never witnessed any miracles in person.

However, his greatest miracle was the hospital he had built in town, in the same place where there was a mountain before. 'That is true', the professor said. 'You are right.' Then he asked me several questions in German about the friar. I answered him, and I spoke in German for almost an hour about Padre Pio. Eventually, I got the highest grade! I always believed that Padre Pio helped me during that exam.

"I saw him for the last time in August 1968, a month before his death. My fiancée and I were about to get married, and we really wanted to get Padre Pio's blessing. I spoke to Fr. Bill Martin, an American monk who was always next to Padre Pio at that time. Bill and I had become friends because he had helped me with some of my English exams. He said, 'I will take care of that. Make sure to be in the hallway of the monastery at seven in the morning.' On that day, we went to the monastery, and we waited, while we were bent on our knees. Padre Pio arrived, unsteady, and leaning on Fr. Bill. As soon as he saw us, he got annoyed. He was not supposed to meet anyone in the hallway. 'What do these two want now?' he asked harshly. Bill replied, 'Father, they are getting married today.' Padre Pio's look on his face immediately changed. His face became endlessly sweet, like a father in front of his children. His eyes were glistening. He raised his hand, he blessed us, and he said, 'Act keeping in mind the holy fear of God!' He believed that the holiness of marriage was an amazing gift.

"Fr. Bill was a great man. His story is beautiful. He came from Brooklyn, New York, and his actual name was William Martin. He was a tall and strong guy, and during the last years of Padre Pio's life, he was a sort of 'bodyguard' for him. The crowd loved Padre Pio, but they were not always delicate, so Fr. Bill protected him, he pushed his wheelchair, and he helped him eat.

"Fr. Bill was born in 1939. He had lost his mother when he was a child, and when he was seventeen years old, his father died, too. He became an orphan then, and he had to run his family business on his own, a funeral home. He was sad; he felt empty and lonely. One day, an English biography of Padre Pio ended up in his hands. He was very impressed by what was going on in San Giovanni Rotondo: the monastery in a small village and this friar that was believed to be a saint. He left New York and moved here to Gargano. When William met Padre Pio, his life totally changed. He quickly learned Italian thanks to Mary Pyle: she was an American billionaire who had arrived in San Giovanni Rotondo in 1923. She later became one of Padre Pio's spiritual daughters. William, however, did not feel completely welcome, and he was thinking about moving back to the United States. But Padre Pio told him, 'You need to stay here!' so William never left San Giovanni, and he became a friar. Guglielmo is the Italian translation of his name, but everybody called him Bill. It was great watching him together with Padre Pio; he was enraptured. He did not move while he stared at him for hours, and he did not say a word, as if he were breathing in the spirituality of that saint.

"On September 22, 1968, Padre Pio celebrated his last Mass. The previous day he had not felt well, but the night had been quiet, so at four in the morning, he went downstairs to the sacristy to get ready, as always. It was Sunday, and there were the celebrations for the fiftieth anniversary of the stigmata. For this reason, delegates from all over the world had arrived. They belonged to the 740 prayer groups that existed back then. The superior of the monastery wanted the Mass to be solemn, that is, sung. It meant it would have been extremely tiring for the celebrant. The church of *Santa Maria delle Grazie* was unbelievably crowded. People were all squeezed in, and there were cameras everywhere. It was hard to breathe. There is a video of that Mass, which shows Padre Pio's pale and suffering face. His voice is shaky, and each gesture is slow, tired, and painful. When it comes to the Preface, he is so exhausted that he can't sing it, so he recites it. Soon after that, he gets lost and recites again the Preface instead of the Our Father. At the end of the Mass, when he gets up from the armchair to go down the steps of the altar, he collapses, he stumbles, and he almost falls down. But Fr. Bill is ready. In the video, you can see him grabbing Padre Pio, holding him strongly, and slowly leading him to the sacristy.

"That night, Fr. Bill was among the ones who witnessed Padre Pio's death in his cell. Later, Fr. Bill studied and became a priest in 1974, under the name Giuseppe Pio. He was available and kind to everyone, and he was always willing to help others. He was loving and humble like Padre Pio. In the 1990s, Fr. Bill had established, here in San Giovanni, a community of believers of the Charismatic Renewal. He thoughtfully took care of them. He was really sweet with sick people, and he used to tell them, 'Hold on; it is a miracle to endure a disease.' He kept repeating what he had always heard from Padre Pio, 'Let yourselves get carried away by God; he knows what you need!'

When he died, a young man who knew him read something at his funeral. He said, 'Fr. Bill, you have been a rescuing angel when we were about to fall, like you did with Padre Pio on the altar.'"

37

He Was Different from the Others

On May 5, 1956, Padre Pio officially opened *Casa Sollievo della Sofferenza*, the hospital he had founded. A big crowd joined the opening, along with some well-known personalities. The cameras of Italian television (RAI) were there, and Tito Stagno was the reporter.

"I met the most amazing people in my life: artists, famous actors and actresses, scholars, national leaders, popes, athletes, astronauts," said Stagno. "I met John Fitzgerald Kennedy, Nehru, President Eisenhower, Pope John XXIII, and Pope Paul VI. But it all started with Padre Pio. I had the privilege of talking with him when I was still a young reporter. I was twenty-six years old, and it was the beginning of my career. I was sent to the opening of *Casa Sollievo* for RAI news. It was an unforgettable experience."

Born in 1930, Tito Stagno is one of the most memorable personalities of Italian television. In the 1960s, and in the 1970s, he was one of the most popular news reporters. He became a legend the night of July 20, 1969, with his report on the landing on the moon. But as he said, one of his first reports was actually about Padre Pio. During the commemoration of that meeting in

Pietrelcina, on November 9, 2019, an award called *Premio Padre Pio* (the Padre Pio Award) was given to Tito Stagno. It is an important and prestigious award that has been given on nineteen occasions. The award was conceived by Gianni Mozzillo and Claudio Crovella, with the support of the association *Amici di Padre Pio* (Friends of Padre Pio). "I usually do not get emotional, but when I received the award, I did. My memories about Padre Pio are really sweet. I joined RAI in 1954, together with Furio Colombo and Umberto Eco. I began with my first reports in 1956, and in May of that year, I was sent to the opening of *Casa Sollievo*. The day before my departure, I had interviewed Gina Lollobrigida in her house on Appia Antica. On that day, she had publicly appealed to help the flood victims of Polesine. When she found out I was about to leave for San Giovanni Rotondo, she told me, 'If you see Padre Pio, do not forget to tell him that I did something good, too, today!'

"I left with the RAI car, together with the cameraman and the sound technician. San Giovanni Rotondo immediately upset me because there was nothing: a few houses, a couple of hotels, and the huge hospital that seemed to come out straight from the mountain. I was staying at the monastery of the friars in a very spartan cell. I was used to my comforts, but there were not any there. In the cell there were just a bed and a sink. There was no hot water. The first morning, we went to the hospital, where we shot pictures in different wards. I remember that the cameraman was a very genuine Roman man. Sometimes, while we were working, he would curse, and the nuns were shocked. It was obvious that we did not belong to that place; we just wanted to do our job well. I did not even know who Padre Pio was. I had done some research, but I was pretty cold and aloof. In the afternoon, after the photoshoot at the hospital, on our way to the monastery, we saw a friar at a window. There were people below that were waving at him with a handkerchief. That was Padre Pio. He came down, towards us. We did not say anything special, but he gently touched my arm. It almost felt like a caress. It sounds weird, but I shivered. In that moment, I realized that Padre Pio was different from everybody else.

"The opening was the next day. Padre Pio celebrated Mass in front of the hospital, at seven in the morning. There were so many people, including the congressman Cesare Merzagora, who was the president of the Senate; Minister Braschi; and the prefect of Foggia. There were also Guglielmo Marconi's widow with their daughter, Elettra; Beniamino Gigli; and Professor Enrico Medi. Cardinal Lercaro, who was the archbishop of Bologna at that time, was also there. Back then, when the priest celebrated the Mass, he did not face the believers. I spent, therefore, the whole time between the altar and the hospital so that I could keep watching Padre Pio. I kept looking at his hands: I had heard about his stigmata, and I was really curious because he used to take off his gloves during Mass. However, the gown he was wearing under his vestment was hiding most of his hands, and I could not see anything. At the time of the blessing, I finally managed to see something, a dark red stain, on the palm of his hand and on its back. Once Mass was over, Padre Pio moved closer to the microphone, ready for his speech. At that point, a setback occurred. The cameraman told me that the film was over, and we could not keep shooting. He needed some new film. I ran then to the microphone, I grabbed it, and I put it on the floor. Padre Pio approached me. He was serious, and he said, 'Man, what are you doing?' I replied: 'Father, if you want your speech to be heard in all of Italy and in the world, not just in this square, you need to be a little patient.' He smiled, and he waited for the cameraman. The audience, however, was not as indulgent as him, and they did not like what I had done.

"Unfortunately, I never met Padre Pio again after that time. I was and I still am agnostic. When it comes to faith, I do not judge anyone, and I am not narrow-minded. But I still remember the way I shivered when he touched my arm, and I always carry that memory with me."

38

The Work of the Soul

Giancarlo Setti, who died in 2002, was the first person in charge of the prayer groups. Padre Pio entrusted him with this task. I had met Mr. Setti in Florence, in the historical center. He was the priest of the church *San Remigio*, and we talked about his friendship with the friar.

"I remember him as a very loving father, ready to help everyone," he said. "Nobody was unhappy after meeting him. That was how he was. Padre Pio was so sweet. He had to help every one of those who asked him, and he used to immediately start praying. He prayed all the time, to thank God for his spiritual children. Padre Pio asked me to help him with the prayer groups, which had just begun. Later, he scolded me for not taking that task seriously."

Mr Setti died a few years after our meeting, which was likely one of his last conversations with a journalist about Padre Pio. He was really nice, and he loved talking about Padre Pio. He tenderly called him "my great friend." I remember he wanted to take me to the small room next to his studio. There was a sort of little chapel in there, dedicated to Padre Pio. There was a bronze bust of him, many pictures, and even some precious relics. In a shrine, there were one of Padre Pio's tunics, a pair of gloves he used to cover the stigmata, and a handkerchief used for stemming the blood that was coming out of his wounded ribs. He explained to me, "In this room, incredible events take place all the time. A lot of people come to me with their big problems that nobody can solve. I take them, then, to this room, and I let them pray alone so that they can privately talk to Padre Pio. His presence is tangible, thanks to these objects that belonged to him. Healings, conversions, and solutions to complicated family issues have taken place in here."

But Mr. Setti did not want to mention the details. At the time of our meeting, the process for Padre Pio's beatification was still underway, and all the necessary material was being collected. Witnesses were asked, therefore, to be discreet.

"One of Padre Pio's main spiritual achievements is the prayer groups. He really cared about them. They were created in the 1950s. If, on the one hand, the hospital *Casa Sollievo della Sofferenza* was his greatest social accomplishment, on the other hand, the prayer groups were his spiritual accomplishment. The two projects were closely related to each other.

"I was a young priest when I visited him for the first time. I had heard people talking about him, and I was really curious. In the newspapers, I had read amazing things about him, but what impressed me were the stories about him told by the people who had met him and who had totally changed because of him. Then, I had heard about the stigmata, and I wanted to check if he actually had the marks of Christ's passion. As soon as I met him, when I was in front of him, there was a spark. I knew he had a big heart, and I could feel his love for everyone, including me. It was such an intense love that you could almost touch it. We did not talk much, but I realized that a big friendship was born. After that time, I often went to San Giovanni Rotondo. It was essential to me.

"Around the end of the 1950s, Padre Pio asked me to be in charge of the prayer groups. I had spent a few days with him at the monastery, and I was ready to go back to Florence. While I was saying goodbye, I added, 'Father, do not forget to pray for me.' He dryly replied, 'You take care of the prayer groups, and I will take care of your soul.' It was basically a deal, a sort of agreement. The prayer groups were something recent. People in all parts of Italy gathered to pray together, following Padre Pio's guidelines. However, they needed to be encouraged and sorted out: that was my job. I had to keep in touch with everyone, to balance the different groups, but I also had to let them have their own specific features. However, I had not actually understood the importance of such a movement. All I did was send a letter of exhortation to the groups once a month. I admit that I was not taking the task seriously, and it was that way for a year. Then, I went back to Padre Pio. I asked him if he had prayed for my soul. His answer was, 'If I took care of your soul the same way you take care of my prayer groups, then you would be in trouble!'

"It was a reproach. He always knew everything. I had to admit that the simple letter I used to send did not show a passionate or diligent job. So I put in more effort. I kept sending my monthly letters, as I did before. But at the same time, I also started visiting the different groups in person. I talked with them, and I gave them Padre Pio's blessing. I realized that I had to be a sort of parent for them; that was what Padre Pio wanted from me.

"As time went by, the groups became bigger and they spread, even abroad. I kept Padre Pio abreast of their activities and progress. It was nice to see how these updates made him happy. Then, 1968 came. It was an important year. On September 20, it was the fiftieth anniversary since the appearance of the stigmata. I decided to orchestrate an international gathering for all the groups so that, on that significant occasion, Padre Pio could be surrounded by his beloved spiritual children. I talked to him about it. We decided that on the 20th, which that year was a Friday, he would celebrate a private Mass. On the 21st and on the 22nd, Saturday and Sunday, he was going to celebrate Mass with the prayer groups. He got excited about that plan.

"It was an unforgettable gathering. Thousands and thousands of spiritual children arrived in San Giovanni Rotondo, together with members of over 700 prayer groups from all over the world. Padre Pio was really touched. I met him several times during those days, but unfortunately, he was not feeling well. He could not be involved as much as he wanted to. On the 21st, he could not even come to church. On the 22nd, he celebrated a solemn Mass for the prayer groups. But once it was over, he was suddenly taken ill, and he was taken back to his cell. We were worried, but we did not think those were the final days of his life, while he was aware that he was going to die.

"On September 22, the day before his death, I went to his room at 10:00 am, and I got his blessing for the last time. I saw him again at 5:30 pm, when he looked out of his window to greet people. I have a picture of that moment, and it is my last memory of him alive: a parent who waves a handkerchief while he says goodbye to his many children."

39

Letters from All Over the World

Tobia Russo was Padre Pio's barber, and he later became one of the postmen of San Giovanni Rotondo. He was sent to work in the area around the monastery, so he was the one who delivered the hundreds and hundreds of letters that came from all over the world to Padre Pio. In order to find out more, I spoke with Claudio Russo, one of Tobia's children. He is fifty-seven years old, and he is a noncommissioned aviation officer.

"My grandfather was a barber, and my father did the same work. When he was eight years old, he was already helping at the shop. When he grew up, he was in charge of the shop, and sometimes he went to the monastery to fix the friars' hair and beard, including Padre Pio. That was how their friendship was born. He used to tell me that Padre Pio had saved him from the German bombs. My dad was a soldier in Pescara. Every time the Germans bombed the city, he hid in an alley near the train station. That hidden area was never affected, but during the last bombing, my father ran to the fields, rather than hiding in the usual alley. He had heard a voice inside of him that said to stay away from the train station. That time, the alley where he used to hide was indeed destroyed by the bombs. My dad told me he was sure Padre Pio saved him.

"Many other episodes prove the friendship between Padre Pio and my father. My dad used to visit him for advice, for his blessing, for a prayer, each time he had to make an important decision. For example, he visited Padre Pio before going to Naples to get surgery for his tonsils. Back then, that surgery was partially risky. But Padre Pio gently gave him a pat on his shoulder and said, 'Do not worry!' Before entering the operating room, my father was surrounded by an intense and pleasant scent. He realized that Padre Pio was next to him, and everything was fine.

"Later, he asked for his advice about when he should get married. He had not even mentioned the name of his girlfriend yet, when Padre Pio patted him and said, 'You are finally helping this girl!' He said this because my mother was an orphan and she did not have a family. Padre Pio already knew everything, even if my dad had never talked to him about it.

"One day, the son of an important manager of an electrical company came to San Giovanni Rotondo by motorcycle. He wanted to visit Padre Pio, so he asked if anyone in the village could take him there. He was sent to my father's shop. The boy explained to him what he was hoping for. My father closed the store and took him to the monastery. He was well-known among the friars, who always let him jump the queue, even if there were many people. My dad and his guest were then standing in the hallway, waiting for Padre Pio. He suddenly smelled an intense fragrance. 'He is here!' he said. 'How do you know?' asked the boy, and then Padre Pio came out from a small door. When he saw them, he stopped. Nobody had said anything yet, but he said to the young man, 'I know you had a long journey with your bike to come here. But I can't absolve you if you do not promise me you will stop being a womanizer!' And he left. The boy was shocked.

"He did not understand how Padre Pio knew about his vice. He told my dad he would be back in a few months, and he was. He went straight to the barber's shop: 'Tobia, could you please take me to Padre Pio?' he asked. They went to the monastery, once again in line in the hallway. When Padre Pio saw them from a distance, he started shouting, 'You need to leave! Go away! You promised me!' The young man became pale. He whispered, 'But how does he know that?' He never came back to San Giovanni Rotondo.

"In 1964, my father stopped being a barber, and he was hired by the postal service. He was in charge of the area surrounding the monastery, so he often had the opportunity to see and talk to Padre Pio. He never had the courage to ask him, but he believed that Padre Pio had something to do with his assignment. Every day, he delivered bags full of letters to him. The letters came from all over the world, asking for his prayers or giving donations for the hospital. My dad was proud and happy because he felt he was helping Padre Pio with one of his projects.

"My great-aunt, my grandfather's sister, was Rachelina Russo. She was one of the first women devoted to Padre Pio, and he wrote many letters to her. These letters, together with others addressed to other spiritual children, were later collected in a volume, one of the most significant mystical books of the twentieth century. It was precisely because of my Aunt Rachelina that Padre Pio came to San Giovanni Rotondo. Only a few people know this story, and it was told to me by the Capuchin monks. Rachelina was a knitter for the friars of the monastery of *Sant'Anna* in Foggia. One day, she met Padre Pio, who had recently moved there from Pietrelcina. He had some lung issues, and the muggy weather of Foggia did not let him breathe properly. Rachelina therefore recommended to the friars that Padre Pio be sent to Gargano, in San Giovanni Rotondo, where she lived. The weather was better there, and Padre Pio would like it. They listened to her, and on September 4, 1916, Padre Pio joined the monastery of San Giovanni, where he stayed for more than fifty years. When I told this story to my father, he started crying. He got emotional when he heard that a member of his family was responsible for Padre Pio's arrival to his village.

"They were good friends. When Padre Pio died in 1968, my father never stopped talking about him. My father passed away in September 2020. During his final days, he kept saying he could see a friar in his bedroom. He told us, 'Move this way because the friar came to visit me.' We had no doubts about who he was talking about."

40

Eel and Turnip Greens

There is a picture of Padre Pio in my archive: he is about to eat some pasta. I think it is a picture from the 1950s. The photographer portrayed Padre Pio during a meal. We can't understand where he is, but it does not look like his cell or the canteen of the monastery. In the background, there is a cupboard with the statue of Our Lady of the Miraculous Medal. Padre Pio is sitting in a little light blue armchair. There is a small table in front of him with a plate and a little beer stein. We are used to seeing pictures of Padre Pio praying, that is, intimate pictures. But when we see him eating, for example, we almost feel embarrassed because it is such a personal and silent moment. At the same time, however, he is very close to us, very sympathetic, and it is a good feeling. I wondered then if Padre Pio had a favorite dish, if there was a food that used to make him happy. For this reason, I spoke with Michele Di Cosmo. From 1946, he was the chef of the monastery of San Giovanni Rotondo for forty years. He also cooked for Padre Pio. Michele di Cosmo is now ninety-three years old. He gets very emotional when he remembers the saint he met, and he has an amazing memory when he describes past events and details.

"Padre Pio liked my large roasted eel, the way I cooked it," he said. "He also liked how I cooked turnip greens and pork livers. When he ran into me, he used to tell me, 'Good job, man!' and I was happy. However, with the exception of these words, he did not give me much satisfaction. Padre Pio did not eat much; he barely tasted the food in front of him. He just ate a crumb, and then he would say, 'It tastes so good!' Then he would push his plate to one of his brothers sitting next to him. He basically never ate; I do not know how he survived. But he was a saint . . .

"I began working at the monastery in 1946 with my brother, Giuseppe. We were handymen at first. We were smart boys, willing to work. We adapted to everything, and we managed to fix every sort of issue. We were in charge of all the maintenance work: we were plumbers, electricians, gardeners, and farmers. Then we started also helping in the kitchen, and we quickly became the chefs of the monastery. I was also in charge of taking the mail for the friars from the post office and then going grocery shopping at the market. Sometimes, with my off-road car, I took Fr. Corrado, who was the treasurer, to the surrounding farms to buy cheese or wheat. We bought genuine ingredients in order to cook simple dishes, typical of our area, that the friars of the monastery really liked. I remember that some friars really had an appetite. One of them, Michele, sometimes walked into the kitchen, and he smelled the aroma coming from the pots. He would smile, satisfied. Then he would grab a plate, pour some sauce on it, and eat it with bread.

"Every morning, my brother, Giuseppe, and I started working at six in the morning. We cooked breakfast, lunch, and dinner for the friars. I often saw Padre Pio, and, occasionally I was sent to his cell to bring him food. It was always crowded. There were his brothers, doctors, friends: they were all there with him, and they always needed his advice. I finished work in the evening, after eight. I did not live in the monastery, obviously, and sometimes, when it was late, I had to walk home because the bus was no longer running.

"When I got to the monastery, early in the morning, Padre Pio was still celebrating Mass. I prepared breakfast for the friars, including coffee, milk, and seasonal fruit, as well as fresh bread, jam, or honey. After Mass, Padre Pio stopped by the kitchen, before his long day in the confessional began. He just drank some milk. He really liked goat milk, so I often bought it from the shepherds of the area. On other occasions, he preferred an herbal infusion rather than milk. His favorite infusion was the one with hundred-knot grass. I picked it from the garden of the monastery. It helped him with his kidneys because it was a detoxifying infusion. Padre Pio never ate anything in the morning because he was in a hurry to get to the confessional. The faithful in line were already there, waiting for him.

"The truth is, as I said, that Padre Pio almost never ate. I tried to cook his favorite dishes for him, but he barely tasted them. He said everything was delicious, but then he moved the plate away from him. He really liked large roasted eel. I cooked it simply, just with olive oil and bay leaves. But he just ate a bite, and that was it. He did the same with other dishes that I know he liked. For example, turnip greens, both boiled and panfried; roasted or barbecued pork livers; and even pasta with tomato sauce, made with the tomatoes from the vegetable garden of the monastery. He really liked buffalo mozzarella, but also in this case, he just had a bite from his knife. It was the same with crème caramel, his favorite dessert. He tasted it, and then he gave it to the person sitting next to him. And the same in the evening, with pasta in broth: a spoonful, and that was it. He even dared to say, 'Stop, I am full!'

"The friars were a little worried because he did not eat, so they came up with an idea. Sometimes they told Padre Pio that a certain dish had been seasoned with the olive oil from Pietrelcina, from the countryside where his parents used to work. Or they would tell him that the peppers had been made with the vegetables from his village that some friends had brought. In this way, they thought they were making him want to eat more because he was always happy to taste the flavors of his childhood. Padre Pio would smile and thank his brothers, saying that the ingredients from Pietrelcina were always the best. But he would still barely taste them, and then he would stop.

"It was nice to see the friars with him in the dining hall. I watched them from the kitchen. Padre Pio was usually late because he was busy with the confessions. According to one of the rules of the monastery, if a friar was late for his meal, he had to bend on his knees and pray, while the other ones kept eating. His brothers knew very well that Padre Pio was late because he was busy at the confessional, so that rule did not apply to him. However, he wanted to be treated like everybody else. If he was late, he bent on his knees, opened his hands, and prayed. Once the prayer was over, he sat at his place on the bench. He was always cheerful with his brothers: he listened to them, and he often shared funny stories. Everybody there knew he was a saint, and they were very respectful towards him. They got close to him, and they asked him for his blessing. He used to reply, 'Go to God because he is the One who will bless you!' But he did not want to disappoint his brothers, so he raised his hand, and he blessed them anyway.

"Sometimes he stayed in his cell because he did not feel well. In those cases, I went upstairs and gave him a bowl with some warm broth. He was never alone. Someone was always with him: a few friars, doctors from *Casa Sollievo*, some friends. I left the bowl on the nightstand, but when it came back to the kitchen, it was still full, so I knew that Padre Pio had not eaten.

"Once, he came to the kitchen while we were working. He walked in silently, holding the rosary in his hand, praying. He looked at us, smiled, and asked us, 'What are you doing, guys?' I told him we were cooking lunch. He nodded, waved, and went back to praying. My brother and I were permanently hired at the monastery, thanks to him. He had personally taken care of it. He had asked the treasurer if our documents were in order. Then he said, 'Hire them, and get their documents in order because they are good boys.' And that was our job for the rest of our lives. During the last years, the friars sometimes asked me to take Padre Pio to the village. It rarely happened; for example, when he went to vote. He did not come with me in my car: he stayed in Dr. Sala's car, who was his personal doctor. I was right behind them, with the wheelchair in my car. When we arrived at our destination, I helped the doctor make Padre Pio sit. He looked at me and thanked me, but his face was discouraged because he did not like using the wheelchair. The friars always kept saying it: that was probably the biggest humiliation for him.

"Many years went by, but I still keep those memories in my heart. I lived next to a saint, a great saint. I get emotional just thinking about the fact he spoke to me. I hope that, when we meet again in heaven, he will remember me and my dishes. It will be amazing to see him again."

41

Wedding with a Miracle

"Padre Pio was one of the most important people I have ever met. I only met him once, in 1962, and then I never saw him again. But it was enough. That time, I witnessed so many incredible events that totally changed my life." These are the words of Gino Latilla, the famous singer from Puglia, who died in 2011 at the age of eighty-seven. I had the chance to meet him and talk about one of his favorite topics: Padre Pio.

Gino Latilla was a star. In the 1950s, he and his wife, Carla Boni, were very famous, a celebrity couple of pop music. Latilla won the Sanremo Festival, as well as the Festival of Canzone Napoletana. He sang songs that were very popular at that time, such as '*Marietta monta in gondola*' and '*Casetta in Canadà.*' He had also sung with the most important artists of that time: Nila Pizzi, Giorgio Consolini, Giacomo Rondinella, and Franco Ricci. In the 1980s, along with Consolini, Pizzi, and Carla Boni, he created a band called *Quelli di Sanremo*, which was very successful. Latilla loved talking about music and his future projects. But he also loved talking about his strange meeting with Padre Pio.

"I had heard about him, I knew who he was, but I was skeptical when I heard stories about him," he explained. "For this reason, I was never keen on going to San Giovanni Rotondo. But in 1962, I went to make a friend happy. Luciano Rispoli, who later became a famous TV personality, was getting married there, and he asked me to come. His uncle knew Padre Pio very well, so he was going to officiate at the wedding. It was therefore going to be a big event.

"We all left a couple of days before the wedding. Since I was curious, I remember that, once we got to San Giovanni Rotondo, I wanted to see the friar everyone was talking about. At 5:00 am, I went to the little church for Mass. It was very crowded. At the end of it, in the sacristy, I was shocked by the number of people in line waiting to be blessed by Padre Pio. Something in particular impressed me: the friar, praying, as if he did not see that crowd patiently waiting for him. I thought it was rude of him, so I got irritated. Rispoli's uncle was devoted to Padre Pio, but for the rest of the day, I argued about this with him and others. But the uncle told me, 'Padre Pio's goal is to save souls. He knows when a person needs to be heard and when it is better to make them wait. If you want, Padre Pio could meet you tomorrow!' I replied, 'I definitely do not want to meet him!' and I stopped thinking about it.

"The following day was the wedding, and Luciano Rispoli gave me the camera and asked me to make a video during the wedding. So in order to shoot, I went up to the choir loft, where the organ usually is. I went through a door, I went upstairs, and I found myself in a hallway. I walked a little bit, I opened a door, and Padre Pio was suddenly there in front of me. He was sitting in an armchair, and he glared at me. He was staring at me, and I could not tell if I was scared or happy. I think I was both. I had mixed feelings. I don't know how long I stayed there, until Padre Pio asked me, 'What are you doing here?' 'I am looking for the organ,' I stuttered. And he said, 'And you are looking for it here? Go away!'

"I closed the door and left. My face was burning. I went downstairs, and I found another hallway. I was worried because I thought the wedding was going to start without me. I saw a small door, I walked in, and Padre Pio was again in front of me. 'Is it you again? What do you want from me?' he said.

"I did not understand what was going on. I was sure I had left Padre Pio upstairs. I apologized and left. I was confused, but I was also partially relieved. If Padre Pio was still there indeed, it meant the ceremony had not started yet, so I was on time. I went downstairs again, I found another hallway, I opened a door, and I was speechless: Padre Pio was there for the third time! 'Maybe I am going crazy,' I thought. But this time, the friar was smiling. There were some kids with him, and they immediately recognized me. 'He is Latilla, the one who sings on the radio!' they said.

"Padre Pio got closer to me. He was looking at me straight in my eyes, and again, I felt emotions that were difficult to describe. It seemed he could see what was on my mind. Then, he raised his right hand covered with the glove, and he hit me three times on my head. They were not caresses but actual blows. And while he was doing so, he told me with his sweet voice, 'Go! Never hurt anyone, and do not be afraid of anyone!'

"Suddenly, I remembered the bride and the groom. I said something to Padre Pio, and I left. I got to the church on time, but no one was there. It was empty. The ceremony was over, but how could that be?! Only a few minutes had gone by after I went upstairs to the choir loft. And upstairs, I had run into Padre Pio three times, so he could not have officiated the wedding. I went outside, and Rispoli's uncle was there. 'Where have you been?' he asked me. 'We have been looking for you everywhere. The newlyweds are already back at the hotel!' 'But who officiated at the ceremony?' I stuttered. 'Padre Pio, of course!' I did not understand; nothing made sense. But I was sure it had happened; it wasn't a dream.

"This is how I met Padre Pio. I never saw him again, but I could always feel his presence next to me. Always. And I never stopped thinking about him."

42

A Foretaste of Heaven

Fr. Francesco Agricola told me, "For my whole life, I held these beautiful memories inside of me. I was lucky enough to see a great saint. I saw him during the Consecration at Mass, and it was amazing because you could see that in that moment he was talking to God. Padre Pio did not forget about me because in 1995, he saved me from the earthquake. If I am here today, it is because of him."

Fr. Francesco is eighty-one years old. He's now retired, but in 1995, when the earthquake occurred, he was the priest of the Fr. Francis of Assisi Church in Ischitella, a small village in Gargano with 4,000 residents.

"On that day, I was supposed to officiate at three weddings. The first one was scheduled at 11:00 am, but the bride was a little late. There were just me, two other priests, and some members of the choir inside the church. At 11:20, the earth quaked. It was a magnitude 7 earthquake, so it was pretty serious. We were all frozen for a moment, and shortly thereafter, the whole roof of the church collapsed on us. I remember shouting 'Padre Pio!' The roar and the dust immediately surrounded me, and then bricks and wood hit me on the head. I felt so much pain. I could no longer see anything. I was yelling the other people's names out, but they did not reply, so I feared they were trapped under the debris. Actually they had survived because they hid in the side choir room, which had been less damaged. I had not moved from the middle of the church, and the collapse had landed directly on me.

"But I was standing; I was alive. My clothes were stained with blood, and there was blood in my eyes, which did not let me see. But I was able to walk, so I moved towards the exit. Outside, people were running away, terrified, and they probably thought that those inside the church had not survived, including me. In a state of a trance, I went to my car, and I drove forty kilometers, all the way to San Giovanni Rotondo, to the ER of *Casa Sollievo della Sofferenza*. I do not know how I managed to drive in those conditions. The doctors were ready, they immediately treated me, and I had some tests done. Once they found out what had happened, they could not believe it. I just had some abrasions, a few wounds on my scalp. I had no serious injuries; I was fine. How could that be possible? The church had collapsed on me, but I was unharmed. I immediately thanked God and Padre Pio. I was, and I still am, sure he was the one who saved me.

"I met him for the first time in 1951, when I was eleven years old. I was about to start the seminary in Manfredonia, and I went to San Giovanni Rotondo with two classmates. The father of one of my friends took us there. We left at night, in order to be there at 5:00 am for Padre Pio's Mass. I remember that, back then, the road to San Giovanni was crooked and unpaved. I remember the crowd inside the church and the complete silence. Padre Pio really cared about silence, and if somebody was making some noise, he would glare at him.

"Mass lasted more than two hours, but nobody seemed to notice that. Everyone was entranced. Padre Pio looked like an old mystic. Each of his gestures had a deep meaning. He made me want to be like him, to celebrate Mass. I was even more determined to become a priest. After Mass, people used to stop in the hallway outside of the sacristy, waiting to be blessed by Padre Pio, to talk to him, and to kiss his hand. When Padre Pio came in front of us, my classmate's dad asked him, 'Is my son going to be a good priest?' Padre Pio said: 'Oh, please, a priest!' That was exactly what he said, a little sharply. It was a strange answer that I didn't understand. But I understood later. He did not become a priest, and actually, he ended up running away from the seminary one night. I found out later that he got married and had two children. Padre Pio's answer of 1951, which sounded so strange back then, later sounded like a prophecy. Its meaning was even deeper because, while my friend did not become a priest, one of his children did. I believe Padre Pio already knew everything.

"I became a priest in 1964. If you were a priest, it was not so easy back then to visit Padre Pio. The Bishop of Manfredonia had forbidden the priests to do so. Part of the Church was against Padre Pio, and they told the worshippers to avoid any contact with him. However, like many other Italian priests, I did not follow those directions, and I secretly went to San Giovanni. It was impossible to stay away from Padre Pio. I can't describe what it felt like being next to him; it was like a foretaste of heaven.

"I used to walk into the church when it was empty, but I knew that Padre Pio was praying in a corner because a beautiful rose fragrance quickly enveloped me. It was a light and delicate aroma. There was always a long line if you wanted to confess to him. You had to book in advance. I remember there was a man from Sicily. He was mad at Padre Pio because for six times in a row, he had sent him away from the confessional. He absolved him only on the seventh time. I found out later that the young man had not mentioned some of his sins to him. But Padre Pio knew about them because he could see inside people's hearts. Sometimes he was the one who listed people's faults, as if they were written in front of him. But often, when he was dealing with serious sins, he wanted the penitents to talk about them first. Otherwise, he sent them away from the confessional. When they were actually sorry for their sins, they went back to him and opened their hearts. Padre Pio absolved them, he hugged them like a father, he got emotional, and he happily smiled.

"I also remember that, during Mass, he took off his gloves, and we could see the stigmata on his hands. They were dark red stains. We knew they were holes that went through his hands. I have always been friends with Fr. Marciano Morra, who was, for a long time, one of Padre Pio's brothers. Father Marciano often told me about the stigmata because he had observed them closely. More than once, he said, 'They were holes.'

"When Padre Pio died, I prayed in front of his coffin and said goodbye before his burial. Everyone was touched in that moment, and we were all looking at his hands. They were amazingly perfect, smooth, clean, and with no scars. It was a miracle."

43

"If You Do Not Want Me Here, I Will Leave."

Engineer Paolo Sala is now sixty-eight years old, and for forty years, he was in charge of all the wiring at the hospital *Casa Sollievo della Sofferenza*. His father was Giuseppe Sala, Padre Pio's personal doctor. He was also the mayor of San Giovanni Rotondo. "My dad saw Padre Pio," he told me. "He also told me about amazing events. For example, he witnessed some bilocation episodes."

Dr. Giuseppe Sala is a figure mentioned and included in all the biographies of Padre Pio. He was born in 1925 and died in 1996, and he was the friar's personal doctor for several years. He was a cardiologist and surgeon, and he had been a student of the well-known Professor Pietro Valdoni. He was recommended by Padre Pio, and he was mayor of San Giovanni for two terms, from 1966 until 1974. Nowadays, the residents of the village still remember him with love.

Engineer Sala added, "I am here thanks to Padre Pio. When I was three years old, I got seriously ill. I was dying. My family asked Padre Pio for help. He told them to not worry because I was going to recover in three days. And he was right. Padre Pio saved me.

"My father came from Merate, in the province of Lecco, while my mother was from Milan. We moved to San Giovanni Rotondo in the late 1950s because he had been offered a job at *Casa Sollievo*. However, the relationship between my family and Padre Pio began with my maternal grandfather, Luigi Ghisleri. He was a civil engineer, and in 1954, he started working on the construction of Padre Pio's hospital. He was the one who asked him to pray for me. When I was three years old, in 1956, following the smallpox vaccine, I contracted bacterial meningitis, and I went into a coma. My father was a doctor, and he knew the situation was hopeless. He called his father-in-law, who was working in San Giovanni Rotondo, at the construction site of the hospital. 'Paolo is dying,' he said. 'Ask Padre Pio to pray for him.' My grandpa immediately went to the friar, and his answer was 'Do not worry. Your son-in-law's faith saved the child. Paolo will get out of bed in three days.' And indeed, three days later, I was totally fine.

"My dad wanted to thank Padre Pio in person. He left for San Giovanni. 'Father, I would like to thank you.' Padre Pio replied, 'Soon we will meet again…' My father thought it was impossible because he worked at the Niguarda hospital in Milan. But a few years later, Professor Valdoni sent him to *Casa Sollievo della Sofferenza* to arrange the equipment, and my father remembered Padre Pio's words.

"In San Giovanni Rotondo, we lived in a house 200 meters (650 feet) away from the monastery. The other kids and I went there every day to play hide-and-seek, and we spent time with Padre Pio. He always hugged me, and he gave me little pictures of saints that he took out of his pocket. He wanted me to be an altar boy so that I could help him during Mass. He officiated at my First Communion. I did not consider him a saint or someone special. He was part of my daily life, and for me, he was a regular friar like others, almost a relative, and I loved him.

"Padre Pio asked my dad to be his personal doctor, and he could not fall asleep at night if he had not been examined. Sometimes, indeed, the friars called at our house, 'Doctor, Padre Pio won't go to sleep unless you visit him. Come quickly to the monastery.'

"My dad also witnessed some bilocation episodes. One night, for example, my father was on his way to work, when he saw a friar walking from the hospital to the monastery. It was Padre Pio, so he called to him. But the friar did not turn around, and he kept walking. The next day, my dad was with Padre Pio. 'I saw you yesterday evening, but you did not answer me,' he said. 'You should have called me more loudly!' he replied. Another night, he found him in our living room. He had heard some noises coming from the wooden rocking chair, so he went to check. He thought it was one of us children, but he saw Padre Pio sitting on the chair. 'Father, what are you doing here?' he asked. 'If you do not want me here, I will leave,' the friar replied.

"One day, on their way back from Naples, my parents had a car accident. Before leaving, my mother had visited Padre Pio, and he had said, 'Poor woman.' These mysterious words impressed my mom. She had no idea that Padre Pio already knew what was going to happen. They were driving at night when they suddenly ran into a combine harvester. It had no lights, and it was abandoned on the road. The crash was terrible. Part of the combine harvester fell on my mom's side, and she was crushed. My father assisted her but realized she had no heartbeat. Then he noticed that my mother's necklace, with a small Our Lady of Lourdes medal, was moving; it was pulsating. He understood that mom was still alive, but he had to take her immediately to the ER. In that precise moment, a car appeared, out of nowhere.

"They drove to the hospital. My mother was seriously injured. She suffered many fractures, and she underwent six hours of surgery. All her jewelry, rings, and necklaces had been removed. A few days later, when my father collected the jewelry and gave it back to my mom, he noticed that the Our Lady of Lourdes medal was missing. 'I never had one,' my mother said. Nobody could ever explain where it came from. They also never found out who was the man in the car that had stopped to take my parents to the hospital. My father never talked about it with Padre Pio, but my father was sure he had something to do with it.

"My dad also used to tell me about the stigmata. He had often examined them as a doctor. He always told me they pierced the hands. Contrary to what some people suggested, it was impossible to believe that Padre Pio had gotten those wounds himself. When Padre Pio died, my father was there, and he was among those who examined his body. He noticed that the wounds had disappeared, without leaving any marks on the skin. It was a clinically unexplainable event."

44

Jesus' Photocopy

On July 28, 2020, the process for the beatification and canonization of Br. Modestino da Pietrelcina, whose real name was Damiano Fucci, officially began, following an edict signed by Fr. Franco Moscone, the archbishop of Manfredonia. Br. Modestino was always believed to be the spiritual and charismatic heir of Padre Pio.

Padre Pio was the one who wanted him in San Giovanni Rotondo. A few days before his death, the friar gave him his own rosary, and he told him, 'Remember, you will always get from me what you need.' Br. Modestino has always been the one who connected people with Padre Pio. All those looking for Padre Pio turned to him first. Several miracles took place thanks to Modestino's intercession, including the two official healings mentioned during Padre Pio's process of beatification and canonization.

Br. Modestino died in 2011, at the age of ninety-four. I had the opportunity to meet him, to talk to him in the monastery of San Giovanni Rotondo. There was a ray of sunshine in his smile: it was Padre Pio. Br. Modestino was his instrument. "Padre Pio make uses of me, in order to help the people who need him," he said. "Every morning, when I wake up, I am willing to help him. He suggests what I need to say to others."

Br. Modestino had a small stature; he almost looked delicate and fragile. But his gaze was like piercing fire. When he spoke to you, he always smiled, and he called you "dear brother." He spoke the dialect of Pietrelcina, the same dialect spoken by Padre Pio. He became more popular after Padre Pio's death in 1968. He became so well-known that every day, hundreds of people went to the monastery and waited in line before talking to him. There were all sorts of people: simple and suffering, poor and well-off. Br. Modestino had something to say to each one of them. He was not a priest because he had not studied theology. He had learned to read and write at an evening school, but his advice was full of wisdom. Even the theologians asked him for his advice.

While we were walking in the vegetable garden of the monastery, where he used to spend time with Padre Pio, he told me, "I was born in Pietrelcina. My mother was one of the peers of Padre Pio's mom. Our families' plots of land were adjoining. I grew up hearing about him all the time. After my military service, I came here to San Giovanni Rotondo to meet him in person, and I realized I could no longer live far away from him. I became a friar, and he was my mentor and my confessor. He loved me. Each time we met, he told me, 'St. Francis will always watch over you.' I was so happy, and I reflected on my happiness.

"Many people wanted to become his spiritual sons and daughters, but they did not have a chance to go to San Giovanni Rotondo. Therefore, in 1956, while I was at the monastery of Agnone, in Molise, I asked Padre Pio if I could meet people on his behalf. He replied, 'Do what you are asking me, and I will help you!' I became his sort of 'spiritual secretary.'

"In 1968, I received an urgent call while I was in a monastery in Isernia. I left immediately, and I arrived in San Giovanni on

September 20. It was a very important date: fifty years had gone by since the first appearance of the stigmata, which occurred on September 20, 1918. After Mass, I went to him. He hugged me, and he was crying. He was holding the rosary in his hands. He gave it to me and said, 'I entrust you with the Holy Rosary. Spread it among my spiritual children.' These were the last words I heard from him. He died three days later. It was like he had officially entrusted me with his spiritual children, scattered all over the world.

"This is why I am here every day, even twelve hours in a row, to listen to those who need Padre Pio. Many believers come to me, and I welcome them, as Padre Pio told me to do. We are an army, and prayers are our weapons. We recite the Rosary every day, all together, even the ones who are far away, because they join us spiritually. We pray for those who suffer, for those who need help.

"During all these years, a lot of people have asked for favors and have gotten them. But it was not up to me. Padre Pio is the one who does everything; I am a tool in his hands. What makes favors possible is people's faith and their prayers. It is not because of me. Every day, people tell me that, surprisingly, they recovered, and they come to San Giovanni to thank Padre Pio. I met many of them. I remember a young man who was in a wheelchair because his legs had been paralyzed for several years. He visited me. He hoped I could ask Padre Pio to help him accept his condition. As always, I prayed to Padre Pio. Some time later, that young man came back to San Giovanni to say thank you. He was no longer in a wheelchair. He had recovered, he walked perfectly, and he could even play soccer. I also remember a little girl from Bolzano. Her parents were very devoted to Padre Pio. She fell from the fifth floor, but miraculously, she was fine. She said that Padre Pio had taken her in his arms, and he had put her delicately down on the ground. What can I say? There are many, many stories. This is what Padre Pio is like. I also feel so much pain that it is difficult for me to sleep at night. But when I sit down here and I know I am doing what Padre Pio told me to do, the pain disappears. I no longer feel anything; I am not even tired. I am actually very energetic.

"Padre Pio was on a mission, and he focused on it throughout his life, with dedication. God chose him and wanted him to be Jesus' 'photocopy,' that is, 'another' Jesus on earth. For all his life, indeed, Padre Pio's body reexperienced Jesus' sufferings. He had stigmata on his hands and feet and a wound on his ribs. After World War II, I often visited San Giovanni, and I helped him with Mass. It could even last two hours.

"I noticed that Padre Pio moved slowly; he cried and sighed. Sometimes, on the skin of his forehead and nape, some small red dots appeared. They looked like thorn stings. And I noticed that Padre Pio kept touching his temple with the finger of his right hand, as if he wanted to lift something that was bothering him. Back then, I could not imagine that, while he was celebrating Mass, he was experiencing the same terrible sufferings that Jesus went through, when the Roman soldiers put a crown of thorns on his head.

"One night, in 1947, he told me that one of his primary sufferings was the one he felt when he changed his vest. I thought the source of that pain was the lesion on his ribs. But it was rather a round bruise, ten centimeters wide, that he had on his right collarbone. It reminded him of the sore on Jesus' shoulder, caused by the wooden cross.

"If you wish to actually understand Padre Pio, you need to be aware of his sufferings. For this reason, Pope Paul VI had called him 'one of God's representatives, with stigmata printed on his body.'"

45

The Politician's Funeral

Padre Pio never forgot about anyone. Engineer Tancredi Falcetto confirmed that. He is eighty-eight years old, and he comes from Ciriè, near Turin. "It did not matter if you only met him once. He looked at you, and he blessed you. And from that moment, he would never forget about you; you were like a son to him. I visited Padre Pio only once, in the 1950s, to ask him for advice. But I felt him close to me my whole life. I turn to him every day, and during the most difficult times, he is next to me. Twenty years ago, for example, he saved my daughter from an accident. He also helped me face some sensitive legal issues."

Engineer Falcetto told me he learned about Padre Pio from his mother, Caterina: "She was devoted to Padre Pio, and she even visited him in San Giovanni Rotondo on several occasions. She kept telling me how impressed she was when she met him in person. He made you be respectful, but at the same time, he was also intimidating. Padre Pio was indeed brusque and grouchy, and his eyes could be on fire. Once, he pointed his finger at my mother, and he shouted, 'Go away!' She was mortified, and she was almost crying, but she realized that Padre Pio was not mad at her but, rather, at a man among the crowd. Padre Pio probably knew something was wrong with him, and in those cases, he was not halfhearted. Padre Pio immediately understood if someone was not confessing a sin or if a person went to him simply out of curiosity. Then he rudely sent them away. But he was willing to forgive them and hug them if they admitted their mistake and came back.

"When I was eleven years old, I witnessed Padre Pio's help for the first time. My godfather was Duccio Galimberti, a hero of the Italian Resistance who was killed by the Fascists in December 1944. My mother, who was already a widow, decided to attend his funeral and to take me with her. It was a very risky situation. We had been warned that the Fascists could arrest Galimberti's relatives and friends that attended the funeral. My mom was worried, but she did not want to give up saying goodbye to Duccio. Therefore, she turned to Padre Pio during her prayers. As Padre Pio always suggested, she had probably sent her guardian angel to him, asking him for help. I am not sure if Padre Pio had anything to do with it, but something strange happened: my mother and I attended the funeral, but we had basically become invisible. Nobody noticed us; we were like shadows, and nobody bothered us.

"I met Padre Pio in person in 1952. I had just finished high school, and I could not decide between engineering and law school. It was an important decision because it was going to affect my future. 'We need to ask Padre Pio!' my mother said. I remember that the church was crowded, and Padre Pio was busy celebrating Mass. You could tell he was special. He radiated something unexplainable, a sort of warmth that you could feel even from afar. I went to Confession, and I disclosed to him my doubts about college. 'Pick Engineering!' he said. And I did.

"That was the only time I visited Padre Pio in San Giovanni Rotondo. But I turn to him every day, when it comes to both important things and smaller things, like if I lose something. If I lose an object, I talk to Padre Pio, and I ask him for his help. And if it is an important object, I always find it eventually. Above all, I tell him about my family, and I beg him to protect them. I know he always has.

"In the 1980s, something unusual occurred, and I am sure he had something to do with it. I was into politics at that time. I had been the mayor of a nearby village, but then I switched to the opposing party. I was decisive, practical, and very fussy. My political opponents made war on me, and they managed to take me to court, accusing me of things I had never done. It was risky, and I was worried, so I thought of Padre Pio. I prayed to him, as if he were in front of me. The following day, I ran into an acquaintance that I had not seen in a long time. 'I heard about your troubles,' he said. 'You should be defended by . . .' and he told me the name of an important lawyer who was also a professor at the University of Rome. He agreed to defend me, and I was totally acquitted. Skeptics say that I ran into the person who told me about the lawyer by chance. But I am sure it was because of Padre Pio.

"Another unusual episode took place in 2001. While my wife, Anna, was at home, she suddenly smelled an intense flower fragrance. She looked around, but she did not understand where it was coming from. In that same moment, our daughter Raffaella Pia smelled the scent, too. The next day, during the carnival parade, someone in the crowd threw a firecracker. It exploded behind my daughter, and it almost hit her in the face. For me, there was a clear connection between the fragrance my daughter and my wife had smelled and the firecracker. I knew that Padre Pio often used the scent of violets to announce his intervention to his followers, and it happened to us, too.

"Ten years ago, we met a young African priest who was studying in Italy. People wanted him to go back to his country because he had hepatitis. But he would not be treated over there, and he could not have continued his studies. It touched us. In prayer, we entrusted him to Padre Pio. For several nights, my wife had the same dream: the Virgin Mary was holding Baby Jesus in her arms, and she was offering him, like a gift. It was a strange dream, and we interpreted it like this: we had to take care of that young priest. We 'adopted' him like he was our son, we had him treated, and he finished his studies. Now he helps the parish priest of a village in Emilia Romagna. I have no doubts that, also in this case, Padre Pio watched over us."

46

"When Are You Going to Bring Me Your Boy?"

Fr. Andrea Livio told me the story of a special meeting with Padre Pio. However, he was not involved in it. The protagonist of the story was his cousin, Silvio Berlusconi, who served as Prime Minister of Italy until 2011.

"Yes, Silvio Berlusconi is really devoted to Padre Pio. When he was a child, he visited him in San Giovanni Rotondo, and he never forgot their meeting. Padre Pio was the one who wanted to meet little Silvio, and he prophesied he would become an important person."

Fr. Andrea Livio is now seventy-five years old, he is a priest, and he has also been an exorcist for the last forty years. He lives near Como. He is one of Berlusconi's distant cousins, and he is very close with him. He told me, smiling, "He calls me 'My Father.' We do not see each other often, just two or three times a year when the whole family gathers in Arcore. On these occasions, we also discuss Padre Pio, and then Silvio asks me to tell him about my job as an exorcist. Silvio is a believer, as is the whole family.

"The Berlusconi family includes twelve nuns and two priests. Silvio's Aunt Marina was devoted to Padre Pio, and she was the one who took him to San Giovanni Rotondo. Marina was the sister of Luigi, Silvio's father. She was a widow, and she was a very religious woman. I think she went to San Giovanni Rotondo for the first time at the end of the 1940s. She was very impressed by that friar with a burning gaze and the stigmata. During Confession, she asked him if she could be one of his spiritual daughters, and he agreed. From that moment, Marina began to regularly go to the monastery of San Giovanni Rotondo. Every year, she stayed there for three months in a row. She became friends with those women who had been close to Padre Pio since the early 1920s. She became especially close with Cleonice Morcaldi. She was Padre Pio's favorite spiritual daughter, and she died in 1986. One day, in 1945, Padre Pio asked Marina to introduce her nephew to him. He said, 'When are you bringing me your boy?' Marina knew he was talking about one of her nephews, Silvio and Paolo, so she replied, 'Father, I have two nephews . . .' 'The eldest, bring me the eldest,' Padre Pio said. The eldest was Silvio, who was nine years old back then. So they planned the trip. I think Silvio's mother, Rosa, also went, and she too became a devotee. Padre Pio listened to the child's confession, and he blessed him in the same way he used to bless his spiritual children, that is, 'Healthy, holy, and old.' Then he said to Marina, 'You have no idea what this child will do. He will become a monarch! He will do great things!'

"Berlusconi never forgot that meeting. He does not often talk about it, and he does not mention any details, but he holds the meeting with Padre Pio in his heart. There are many pictures of the friar at his house, but there is a special one. It is in a silver frame, with an inscription on its back, written by Padre Pio for him. Throughout the years, Silvio went to San Giovanni Rotondo several times, even recently. When he is in the area for work, he always stops by for a visit. He is always very discreet, almost incognito—partly because he does not want to be photographed or interviewed by the journalists but, above all, because he considers those visits personal and private, and he doesn't want to share them with anyone.

"For a few years, Silvio and I grew up together. During the war, his family moved to Oltrona, the village where I was born, in the province of Como. Then they moved to Milan. I remember he was very smart, and he was really good at school. His lowest grade was an A. He always had a big heart. Everyone knows about Silvio's generosity, but people only see part of it because he does not want to get a lot of publicity. I remember something that happened in 2001. Berlusconi entrusted me and others with the delivery of a donation to *Pio Albergo Trivulzio*, the famous nursing home in Milan for poor and old individuals. It was a donation of one billion lire (about $500,000)! I never forgot it.

"I never met Padre Pio, and I am very sad about it. I remember people from my village that were devoted to him, and they got emotional when they talked about him. When I was a priest in Como, a lady came to me, and she told me something unbelievable. She wanted to confess to Padre Pio, but he had sent her away. The same thing kept happening, and the third time, Padre Pio shouted, 'First, you throw away your lover's letter in your pocket, and then you dare come here!' He knew everything; he could read people's hearts. I have been an exorcist for almost forty years. Fr. Carlo Barera, the well-known exorcist from Lecco, who died three years ago, asked me to do it. Padre Pio knew him. One day, a priest from Lecco had taken some people to Padre Pio. When Padre Pio found out where they were from, he asked them, 'Why did you come here? Fr. Barera lives close to you. You should visit him!' Even Padre Pio knew about his great charisma."

47

The Child and the Saint

I wanted to keep my conversation with Sergio Rendine for the final chapter. I thought it would be the perfect ending to this collection of memories. I rarely got so emotional hearing a story about Padre Pio. I was like a child, listening to an amazing fairytale told by his grandfather.

The story told to me by Rendine is actually from the point of view of a child. From six to fourteen years old, he lived in the monastery of San Giovanni Rotondo, always next to Padre Pio. He kept Padre Pio company, they ate together, and he could go upstairs to his cell whenever he wanted. He saw and heard many things. He was a spectator, and he recorded every detail in his mind. Rendine's memories are very clear. They are also so incredibile that they leave you speechless. His portrayal of Padre Pio is intimate, caring, but even blazing when he describes his charismas.

Sergio Rendine does not really care to talk about his job as a musician. He does not like being the center of attention, and he prefers to let the music talk. But he has a lot to say. He is in fact considered one of the greatest contemporary composers of classical music and opera. His resume is impressive. He was only four and a half years old when he performed his first Beethoven concert at the San Carlo theater in Naples. He got his Composition diploma from the Conservatory in Rome, and another one in Choral Music and Conducting from the Conservatory in Pesaro. He worked for La Scala in Milan, the Opera in Rome, the Arena of Verona, the National Academy of Santa Cecilia, the Bolshoi in Moscow, the National Symphony Orchestra in Prague, and the Florida Orchestra of St. Petersburg. He created music for the BBC and RAI. In 1995, he was invited by the Nobel Peace Prize organization to compose the "Alleluia," performed at the end of the ceremony in Oslo. In honor of Padre Pio, he composed the official Mass for his beatification. He could have told me about international events or his personal achievements, but Rendine preferred instead to tell me about his friendship with Padre Pio. 'Because he was the most important thing that happened in my life,' he said. 'I met him for the first time in 1960, when I was six years old. Even on that occasion, I witnessed a miraculous recovery: my father's.'

Rendine's father was Furio Rendine, the legendary author of Neapolitan songs. He wrote them for Claudio Villa, Aurelio Fierro, Nunzio Gallo, and Marisa del Frate. He was a friend of Padre Pio.

I went to see Sergio Rendine at the monastery of Moscufo, near Perugia, where he has been living and working for many years. His days are punctuated by music and prayers. His current lifestyle is completely different from his past. He told me about this change, and he explained to me that it took place thanks to Padre Pio.

"I began living next to Padre Pio, in the monastery of San Giovanni Rotondo, when I was six years old until I was fourteen. My father was one of his spiritual sons, and as soon as school was over, he took me to him. I used to spend the whole summer at the monastery. I had my own little room, and my schedule was the same as the friars. I ate with Padre Pio, I often stayed in his cell until late, and I fell asleep there, while he was praying or while he was busy answering the several letters he received. He used to call me 'Sergitiello,' and he taught me catechism in the silence of the garden of the monastery. He always wanted me next to him, so I witnessed amazing things, many of those miracles that took place daily, when he was around.

"My dad had a bad car accident in 1959. He survived, but his femur was broken in eight different places. One of his legs became five centimeters (two inches) shorter than the other, and his knee was hopelessly stiff. My father had to use a walking stick. However, he was sure Padre Pio had saved him from death, so he wanted to go thank him in person. It was the first time my father was meeting him in person, and I went with him. I remember the friar blessed us, and my dad bent in front of him, without noticing he could easily bend his stiff knee. He left the room without using the walking stick. Only a few minutes later, he realized what had happened, when Fr. Onorato Marcucci, Padre Pio's assistant, ran after him with the stick in his hand. 'Furio!' Fr. Onorato shouted. 'Furio, you are walking without this!' My father stopped for a moment, and then he understood: like a child on Christmas morning, he started running in the monastery, upstairs and downstairs, screaming with joy.

"The next day, he went to the hospital, *Casa Sollievo della Sofferenza,* bringing the x-rays of two weeks earlier with him. He had some more x-rays done, and the radiologist compared them. 'Are you sure we are examining the same patient?' the doctor asked. 'There were eight bony calluses in the femur in the first x-rays, but in today's x-rays the bone looks intact!' My father was shocked, so he added, 'I bet it is your first time here in San Giovanni Rotondo. Padre Pio lives nearby, so we are now used to these things!'

"I ended up getting used to it, too. Padre Pio was a mysterious man, and at first, I was even scared of him. He was 'the good boogeyman' for me. He intimidated me. When I was five years old, I stopped breathing when I saw him. His skin was as light as marble, his beard was pure white, and his eyes could pierce you. It seemed there was a bright aura around his face. When he walked, he shuffled. Because of the stigmata on his feet, he could not lift them, lower them, or bend them, like we all do when we walk. Therefore he shuffled. You could hear him coming because of the noise his feet made: it was a regular and slow sound. His voice was deep. Sometimes his manners were brusque. He really made me feel uncomfortable. But then, he would look at me, smiling, and he would look like a child I could play with. Padre Pio was an atypical man, almost an alien, and at the same time, he was childlike, a playmate.

"When he was with me, he behaved like a child. I was always with him at the monastery. He told me jokes, and sometimes we innocently pranked his brothers. For example, he told me, 'Sergitiello, come here; we are going to prank Fr. Onorato. Grab that piece of fabric and put it under his tunic, and then shout, 'A mouse!' I did so, and Fr. Onorato ran away, while Padre Pio laughed.

"He taught me catechism. It was just the two of us, in the vegetable garden of the monastery. I sat on his knees or next to him on the ground. Once, when I was six years old, I asked him, 'Why did Jesus have to go to hell before resurrecting?' He sweetly replied, 'Sergitiello, have you ever thrown a paper ball using the spring of the pen? You take the spring of the pen, and you put the paper ball on top of it. If you want to throw it, you need to push the spring down. When you let it go, the paper ball flies in the sky.' This was Padre Pio's explanation; I still remember it. If you want to reach the sky, you need to go down first.

"Next to the porch, in front of his cell, there were a few wicker armchairs, where Padre Pio used to sit to rest and entertain guests. There was also a little wicker chair made just for me. I was always there, the whole summer. Sometimes my parents came to the monastery because they were both devoted to Padre Pio. They spent some time at the village, and then they went back to Naples. Sometimes my father came with his friends, such as Carlo Campanini. My dad and Campanini tried to persuade Walter Chiari to visit Padre Pio, but they never convinced him. But once, Sergio Bruni, the famous Neapolitan singer, came with my father. I remember that meeting very well. Bruni was kind of full of himself, so when he arrived in San Giovanni Rotondo, he was convinced that everyone would recognize and applaud him. He went to church with my father. He kept asking my dad the words of the 'Ave Maria' in Latin. All morning, Bruni learned those words. In the afternoon, they visited Padre Pio. Bruni introduced himself.

'Father, I am Bruni (which also means "brown" in Italian)!' he said.

'Well, I am white!', Padre Pio replied.

'Father!'

'Yes?'

'I would like to sing Schubert's 'Ave Maria' for you!'

'How can you sing it if you do not even know the words?!'

"Padre Pio showed him he knew he had spent the entire morning learning the words of the prayer. The singer was very impressed. After that, his personality changed, and he became devoted to Padre Pio, too.

"I had my own little room at the monastery, like the friars. At the beginning, I used to sleep in the same room as Fr. Eusebio Notte, who, back then, was one of the friars who took care of Padre Pio day and night. I remember that I was scared of the monastery when it was dark. It became a little disturbing at night:

there was not much light, just a few oil lamps and some candles in front of the holy paintings. Then, the pendulum clock interrupted the silence. This is why I was afraid to sleep alone, and I therefore with Fr. Eusebio. A few years later, when I was older, they gave me my own room. My schedule was the same as the friars. They told Padre Pio I was still a child, and perhaps it would have been too demanding, asking me to wake up in the middle of the night to go to church. But Padre Pio replied, 'No, no, Sergitiello will do what we do!' So I used to wake up at night with the friars, and I joined the choir. When I was five years old, I learned to read the notes on the stave. When Padre Pio celebrated Mass, I was there, next to him. Then, he had breakfast, and later he went to the confessional.

"I remember well when Padre Pio came downstairs for morning Mass. He was a different person, totally distant from everything else. He was no longer there because he was completely focused. He was absent. If someone had set fire to his beard during those moments, he would not have noticed it. It was amazing how he could endure some physical efforts. During Mass, for example, he held the host up for thirty minutes, with his arms still and stretched. It was the same with the goblet. When Mass was over, he spent twenty minutes expressing his gratitude. Little by little, you could tell he was regaining consciousness: he breathed deeply, he touched his beard, and he slowly made contact with the surrounding environment.

"He did not talk much in the cafeteria. He was the first one who walked in, he was jolly with the other friars, and he talked a little bit with them. Everyone was aware he was a saint, so they always asked him to be blessed. He used to answer, 'God is the one who will bless you!' But he blessed them anyway. Then he sat on the end of the table, and I sat next to him, side by side.

"He really loved crème caramel. He took a little bit with the teaspoon, he tasted it, and he gave me the rest of it. I had a sweet tooth, so I quickly ate everything. He loved buffalo mozzarella for lunch. They gave it to him, and he took a little piece with the tip of the knife. 'It tastes so good,' he said, but he gave me the rest of it. It was the same in the evening, when it came to pasta. Padre Pio basically never ate, while I ate for both of us. He did not eat, and he did not sleep. I often fell asleep in his cell, and the friars later picked me up. He kept praying, and then he went to the table to answer to all the letters he used to receive—tThe whole night. Then he lay down for an hour, and later he got ready for Mass.

"He had a little snuffbox. It was useful because it helped him breathe better. When somebody with his same habit was around, Padre Pio offered them his snuff. This happened especially with my father. One day, my dad decided to keep some of the snuff as a relic, so when Padre Pio offered him some, he took a lot of it. With his fingers, he dug deeply in the little snuffbox, leaving a hole.

'Furio, do you know where your father is buried?' Padre Pio asked him. My dad did not know because his father died in Turkey during the war, but nobody knew where.

'I think so,' my dad said.

'Then why did you dig this grave?' he asked, pointing at the little box.

"A journalist from a magazine wrote that Padre Pio's stigmata appeared because he thought too much about it. Padre Pio said to one of his brothers, 'Fr. Pellegrì, write back to this journalist and tell her that if she really keeps thinking about an ox, a pair of horns will appear!' I was there when Padre Pio said this.

"I am one of the few persons who did not simply see Padre Pio's stigmata, but I even held them in my hands. One night, Padre Pio was sick, and he had a very high temperature. He was in bed, and Fr. Onorato was next to him. He was cleaning the wound on his right hand, using some cotton wool. I was with them in Padre Pio's cell, sitting in a corner. I was eleven. At some point, somebody came and called Fr. Onorato because they needed him on the phone. Fr. Onorato gave me the cotton wool, and he said, 'Sergio, keep doing it.' I was a little disturbed. But I slowly grabbed Padre Pio's hand while he was sleeping. I could see very well that there was a hole, and you could see through it. Fr. Onorato came back then, and he kept taking care of him.

"One day, a lady came with a little girl who was paralyzed, in a wheelchair. She was probably ten. I was there, and the lady said, 'Father, could you pray for my little girl?' He answered, 'This little girl is beautiful! But what happened? I bless you, dear daughter, and do not worry because God will help you.' The girl suddenly stood up, ran, and hugged Padre Pio.

"On another occasion, I was with him in the little living room where he welcomed his friends. Someone came to let him know that a French lady had arrived, and she was hoping to meet him. She had walked from France, barefoot, to ask Padre Pio to save her son, who was really sick. She was exhausted, her clothes were torn and dirty. Her feet were bleeding. Padre Pio got mad. 'You can't do this kind of thing!' he shouted. 'You can pray to God from your home. There is nothing I can do!' He meant it was impossible for him to get from God the healing of her son. The woman was bent on her knees, crying. He softened, he told her to stand up, and he looked at her feet. 'Look at you,' he said. He bent and waved his hand, as if he wanted to take the dust off her feet. Then he blessed her and left. He left me behind. I looked at the woman's feet, and I noticed they were totally fine and clean, like she had just had a pedicure.

"A further episode I remember concerned a lady from Asti. She visited Padre Pio because she had cancer, and she was desperate because she had four children. I heard her asking Padre Pio to heal her. 'No,' he said. 'Dear daughter, you will not recover, but you will keep living!' This woman had metastases in all the main organs, but she only died eight years ago. She was not taking any drugs.

"When I was twelve years old, I saw Padre Pio performing an exorcism on a possessed woman called Dina, from Turin. My father, together with a few friars and an exorcist named Fr. Raimondo, decided to take Dina to the cave of Monte Sant'Angelo in order to perform an exorcism. Dina was a tiny woman, but four men needed to restrain her. My father and the others walked into the cave with Dina, while my mother, my sister, and I stayed outside. But I was too curious. I ran away and followed them. I hid myself behind a column, and I saw everything. The woman was screaming so badly that she sounded like an animal. They could barely hold her. My dad, Fr. Pancrazio, Fr. Daniele, and Fr. Raimondo, who was blessing her, were there. I saw with my own eyes that this woman was walking upside down on the vault of the cave, like a spider. Then she jumped like a monkey. The exorcism seemed to be useless. Their last possibility was to call Padre Pio. They planned everything. They went to San Giovanni Rotondo, and I was with them. The church was closed, and only a few candles on the altar were lit. The woman was in the center, surrounded by all the others, who were trying to hold her. She was screaming so loud. At some point, we heard Padre Pio's footsteps. When he arrived, Fr. Eusebio and Fr. Onorato were supporting him. He moved in the middle between the woman and the altar, so the candles cast his shadow on the ground. When his shade 'touched' her, she started shaking, and she fainted.

"A few seconds later, she was perfectly fine. Padre Pio turned to the friars and said, 'Did you call me just for this?' And then he left.

"Another time, I went to the monastery for the Christmas holiday. I was in the hallway with Padre Pio. He stopped and looked up, thrilled. 'Sergitiè! Look! Can you also see the Virgin Mary with Baby Jesus?' 'Actually no, Father,' I said. 'Come on, do not make fun of me!' he said. He really thought I could see her, too.

"A peculiar thing that I have never mentioned before also took place, something incredible. I witnessed it, and I can just describe what I saw with my own eyes.

"I do not remember what year it was. A friar of the monastery had died. I think his name was Maurizio or Daniele, but I am pretty sure he was not a priest, so he was not 'Father.' I was in the little living room, with Padre Pio and other people, including my father. Somebody came to inform Padre Pio of this death that had occurred at the hospital *Casa Sollievo*. When he heard the news, I saw Padre Pio burst into tears. He was inconsolable, and I realized he was very close to that brother. He was sobbing, and I heard him saying, 'Why? Why?' Then he suddenly said, 'Take me to him!' We all stood up and went to the hospital. Even though *Casa Sollievo* was near the monastery, we went by car because that day it was pouring rain. My dad and I were in one car, while Padre Pio and other friars were in another one. More people came instead on foot, underneath the rain. We walked into the funeral parlor. The body of the friar was covered with a sheet, except for his face. I remember his red beard. Padre Pio was offered a chair to sit on. He kept crying. He was rocking his body, back and forth, as if he was rocking his lifeless friend. Then he dried his eyes with a handkerchief and said, 'Leave me praying alone.' We all left and went to the waiting room. It was so silent. Nobody spoke; we barely breathed.

"I do not know how much time went by, maybe a few minutes, but suddenly the door opened. Padre Pio was there, happy and smiling. The friar that had recently died was with him. But he was now standing up, alive. I clearly saw him. His body was wrapped in the sheet, and he made me think of the old Romans. Everyone fell on their knees, wide-eyed. The friars quickly sent everybody away, including me and my father, and they closed the door behind them. Something shocking had just happened, right in front of me. But in that moment, I didn't realize it. I actually understood what happened only later, when I was older, and I thought again about it. I jealously kept my memories. I never attempted to explain what had happened because only faith could explain it. What I witnessed belongs to the group of experiences I lived when I was next to Padre Pio, together with his teachings, his words, and his gestures.

"For some time, however, I forgot about my childhood with Padre Pio, as if it never happened. It seems that our life has already been established for us, even before we are born. But there is something really evil in people's lives that can change and divert it. The adults in my family had already decided that I was going to enter the seminary when I was fourteen years old. They were sure of it. I don't know if Padre Pio agreed with them; I did not hear him talking about it. But when I turned fourteen, I definitely did not want to enter the seminary. I was very clear with my mother. I liked girls, and I was not going to become a priest. I was determined; I would have never been chaste.

"So I kept studying, I went to high school, and I got my music diploma. I started having my first girlfriends. My lifestyle was very distant from the Church. I did think about Padre Pio, but he was on the sidelines. I was somehow resigned to live the way I lived. It sounds like an excuse, but it is the truth. There were no rules in my life. People that do my job can even have ten women in a month. Drugs are very common, and if you do not take them, you look like an idiot. And then the villas, nice cars, lovers, and power: for several years that was my life.

"In the meantime, however, some events occurred that tried to steer me in a different direction. I was called to attend Padre Pio's beatification Mass. It was definitely not my idea. That was when clearer memories began to resurface. I asked myself, 'What kind of life am I living? What would Padre Pio say?'

"It was not accident that the most significant things I did had to do with the Church. For example, Padre Pio's beatification Mass, *Passo et Ressurectio* for Good Friday of the Jubilee in 2000, and the song for John Paul II's twenty-year anniversary. I told myself, 'I have lived among the saints!' I met Padre Pio; Daniele Natale; Fr. Pancrazio, the founder of the House of Bethany; Mother Speranza; Fr. Dolindo Ruotolo. John Paul II . . . I was really an idiot to live the way I lived! Padre Pio came back into my life. He was so amazing and caring with me. I was asked to create something for his beatification Mass. I wanted to focus on his life, and I wanted to create something to be performed on stage, something that glorified him, explaining how he had lived and what he had done. I remember very well that I was taking a shower, and I was thinking about my project, when I clearly heard someone talking. 'Sergitiè! What are you doing? Do you really want to take me on stage? Are you crazy?' I was motionless, all wet, and Padre Pio was talking to me. He was helping me realize I had to focus on something different. So I thought of working on a Mass for him.

"Finally, a few years ago, I had a dream about Padre Pio. He told me: '*Uagliò! Mò t'avimmo fatto pazzià fino a mò. Mò ha de turnà a casa.*' (We allowed you to have fun so far, now it is time to go back home.) I thought he was talking about my death. But no, he wanted me to be part of the Church again. And that is what I did; I live in a monastery now."

the WORD among us®

The *Spirit* of Catholic Living

This book was published by The Word Among Us. Since 1981, The Word Among Us has been answering the call of the Second Vatican Council to help Catholic laypeople encounter Christ in the Scriptures.

The name of our company comes from the prologue to the Gospel of John and reflects the vision and purpose of all of our publications: to be an instrument of the Spirit, whose desire is to manifest Jesus' presence in and to the children of God. In this way, we hope to contribute to the Church's ongoing mission of proclaiming the gospel to the world so that all people would know the love and mercy of our Lord and grow more deeply in their faith as missionary disciples.

Our monthly devotional magazine, *The Word Among Us*, features meditations on the daily and Sunday Mass readings, and currently reaches more than one million Catholics in North America and another half million Catholics in one hundred countries around the world. Our book division, The Word Among Us Press, publishes numerous books, Bible studies, and pamphlets that help Catholics grow in their faith.

To learn more about who we are and what we publish, log on to our website at www.wau.org. There you will find a variety of Catholic resources that will help you grow in your faith.

Embrace His Word, Listen to God . . .